Acknowledgements

Active Parenting Today is based on the time-tested theories of some of the great psychologists of the twentieth century. Chief among them are two Austrian psychiatrists who, though now deceased, continue to exert a profound influence on how we can effectively parent our children. Their names are Alfred Adler and Rudolf Dreikurs. I respectfully acknowledge that their contributions lie at the heart of this program.

Complementing the theories of Adler and Dreikurs, I have included communication skills that have grown out of the pioneering work of Carl Rogers, Robert Carkhuff and Thomas Gordon. I am also indebted to the work of Haim Ginott, Albert Ellis and Milton Erickson.

I also acknowledge and thank my two mentors, Professor Kenneth Matheny of Georgia State University and Professor Oscar Christensen of the University of Arizona. You are much more a part of this program than the one story that I "borrowed" from each of you. Thanks are also expressed to Professor Roy Kern of Georgia State University, who first introduced me to parenting education some 20 years ago, and to Frank Walton, who just keeps on encouraging.

Finally, I would like to acknowledge the tremendous work of the staff at Active Parenting Publishers, who continue to make the dream of Active Parenting a daily reality. A special thank-you to Lisa Wasshausen, Nancy Ballance and Jim Polak, our product development team, who saw this project through to completion. And to a very special employee of the company, my father, Harry G. Popkin—social worker, camp director, role model and inspiration. It's been great working with you, Dad.

Michael H. Popkin
Atlanta, Georgia

Photographs by Julie Fletcher and Tom Hurst

Table of Contents

Preface

Michael H. Popkin, Ph.D.

Active Parenting Publishers, founded in 1980, created the world's first video-based parenting education program. The need for such an innovation in parenting education was based on two beliefs about parenting in our modern democratic society:

1. Parenting well is extremely important.
2. Parenting well is extremely difficult.

It is also assumed that most parents want to parent well, but have not been given the necessary skills or support to parent well.

This lack of training can be disastrous in our modern society, where children openly reject traditional parenting methods. Everywhere, we find parents and children engaging in frustrating struggles for power. Families often become an energy drain and source of frustration rather than a support network and source of satisfaction. Worse, many children are not developing the basic qualities necessary for thriving in our modern society: courage, responsibility, cooperation and self-esteem.

Consequently, many parents of young children express fear about the choices their children will make when they become teenagers. This fear may be well-founded. Teenage drug use, pregnancy, abortion, crime, AIDS and suicide all remain at frighteningly high levels.

Obviously, parenting is not the only influence on a child's development, but it is the one we can do the most about. This *Parent's Guide* has been designed to teach you a method of parenting and problem solving that will help you prepare your children to courageously meet the challenges life will pose. And it will help you build relationships that bring joy and satisfaction for a lifetime.

> *At the end of our lives, we will not remember how much money we made, how many ball games we watched, or how many things we possessed. What will come back to us in a brilliant and blinding light is the quality of the relationships we formed with those we loved: our friends, our spouses, our children.*

Courage and Fear

Courage first met fear
When I was still a child;
Courage gazed with cool, clear eyes;
Fear was something wild.

Courage urged "Let's go ahead;"
Fear said "Let's turn back."
Courage spoke of what we had,
Fear of what we lacked.

Courage took me by the hand
And warmed my frozen bone;
Yet fear the while tugged at my legs
And whispered "We're alone."

Many have been the obstacles
Since first I had to choose,
And sometimes when courage led me on
I've come up with a bruise.

And many have been the challenges
Since fear and courage met,
And yet those times I've followed Fear,
Too often—tagged along Regret.

– Michael H. Popkin

The Active Parent

Perhaps the truest thing that can be said about parenting is that it requires a lot of energy. It is a tremendously "active" undertaking. In fact, it is very difficult to parent well from a sitting position. Children, it seems, respond better to actions than to words. And so, to be an effective parent is to be an active parent. This is one of the reasons we have chosen the name *Active Parenting Today* for this course.

We also want to think of the word "active" as a contrast to the "reactive" approach used by most parents. Reactive parents wait until their children push them to their limits, then they react. Often they react with frustration, anger and random discipline . . . or as one mother put it, "the screech and hit" school of parenting.

When parents "react" rather than "act," they are allowing the child to control the situation, as well as the parent's own emotions. Problems tend to continue or even get worse as parent and child re-act the same frustrating scenes over and over.

Our philosophy in Active Parenting Today *is that it is the job of the parent, rather than the child, to play the leadership role in the family.*

Part of the problem is that most parents do not have a consistent approach to parenting. They use a little of what their parents did, a little of the exact opposite of what their parents did, and a little they picked up from friends, books and magazine articles. Our philosophy in *Active Parenting Today* is that it is the job of the parent, rather than the child, to play the leadership role in the family. This course will help you clarify your own goals for your child and teach you effective methods for leading your child towards them. But it will do more. It will also teach you a consistent model of parenting, enabling you to act with confidence and clarity as you encounter the many challenges parents face.

There are other reasons why we chose to emphasize the word "active." This is an age of active people, who are engaged in a host of active pursuits: jobs and careers, community work, political causes, the arts, hobbies and sports. The fact that you enrolled in this program shows that you are one of these active people; you are taking steps toward improving your family interactions, and you are seeking information to help you excel as a parent. So this workshop is for active people like you.

This program is also "active" in another sense. It uses learning methods that call for the active involvement of all participants. Active learning is effective learning, and we believe we have developed a parenting program that uses the most effective learning approaches available. First, *Active Parenting Today* uses the combined power of video presentations and group interactions in the classroom setting. We think you will find that you can become involved actively in such a process—that you can absorb information, sharpen your insights, hone your ideas, and share them with others in a process that will become dynamic for you. Second, we have fun with group learning exercises in which every participant can take an active role. And third, we make use of this *Parent's Guide*.

This *Parent's Guide* is a resource providing you with useful information and practical skills. Most parents find it helpful to review key concepts in the *Parent's Guide* from time to time. The *Parent's Guide* also contains activities for use at home and in your group. These activities will strengthen your ability to use the skills of *Active Parenting Today* and are an important part of your learning experience.

A word of caution: During the next six weeks, you will learn a very practical model for understanding and leading children. This model, based on the work of psychologists Alfred Adler and Rudolf Dreikurs and expanded by others, has been used effectively by more than a million parents, counselors, teachers and psychologists. It works! However, it is put into use by human beings, and human beings, as we all know, are imperfect. We make mistakes. During this workshop you will probably become aware of two kinds of mistakes of your own:

■ **First**, you may realize or recall mistakes you have made in your own parenting in the past. Almost everyone does. It is important that you recognize these mistakes, but it is much more important that you let them go. They are in the past, and it is useless to dwell on them now. It's much more productive to concentrate on being a more effective parent in the present!

■ **Second**, you will make further mistakes as you learn these new skills. Mistakes are part of the learning process, and they happen to everyone using new skills. So it is important that you accept your mistakes without punishing yourself for being imperfect. If you are too hard on yourself, you not only make yourself feel bad, you also put limits on your learning. This is because when we feel criticized, even by ourselves, we become defensive. Soon we don't even admit our mistakes to ourselves, and we lose the valuable opportunity to correct and improve our performance. Mistakes are for learning; please be kind to yourself!

Parenting: The Most Important Job

Parenting, though still one of the most underrated jobs in our society, is now beginning to attract some of the attention and consideration it deserves. After all, if the future of our society is our children, then the key to that future rests primarily with parents and teachers. Many schools, religious institutions, mental health centers and other community organizations are responding to this reality by offering support to parents through programs such as *Active Parenting Today*.

The Purpose of Parenting

The basic purpose of parenting has not changed. We can state it like this:

> *The purpose of parenting is to protect and prepare our children to survive and thrive in the kind of society in which they live.*

Although this purpose has not changed over the years, the society in which we are living has. For one thing, it is more dangerous. The illegal drugs available to today's children and teens are easier to find and more harmful than ever. Crimes against children—and crimes by children—are more numerous than when we were growing up. There is a serious problem with guns in schools, and even sex can now be life threatening. This poses a difficult problem for parents. Part of our purpose as parents is to protect our children so they will survive. Yet if we overprotect them, we are not preparing them to survive and thrive on their own. Keep in mind that the job of parenting is to work yourself out of a job! That means preparing your child for independence. Three things will help:

1. Talk with other adults to get an idea of what risks are reasonable for your child to take in your community.

2. Join with other parents—through your child's parent-teacher

association, parent support groups, or other organizations—to work within your community to make it a better place to raise children.

3. Allow your child to develop independence gradually. *Active Parenting Today* will help you learn the skills that will encourage your child to build independence. Because children develop through various stages, appropriate behavior at one age may not be appropriate at another. There are many good books available to help you know what to expect at these ages and stages of development. Talking with your child's teachers and other parents will help you, too.

A Society of Equals

If the bad news about modern society is that it has become more dangerous, the good news is that it has also become more just. We can be proud that our country was founded on the principle that all people are created equal. In fact, this concept of equality is a hallmark of democratic societies throughout the world.

Unfortunately, the word "all" in the United States of America in 1776 really meant all white males who owned land. The rest were not even allowed to vote. But the ball of social progress was moving, and during the next 150 years such milestones as the end of slavery, the beginning of the labor movement and the right of women to vote showed that we intended to fulfill the promise of democracy. Then, in the 1950s with the advent of television, the movement for social equality took a giant leap forward. When Martin Luther King, Jr. spoke of his dream of equality for all humankind, the television cameras carried his message throughout the world. One group after another—African-Americans, Native Americans, Hispanics, Asians, students, women—began to demand that they, too, be treated as equals. Today, no group is willing to be treated as inferior, to unquestioningly do what they are told, to speak only when spoken to, or otherwise allow themselves to be treated disrespectfully.

The atmosphere of equality in which our children live has created a new challenge for today's active parents. We must now contend with a generation of children who no longer accept *their* traditional role of inferiority in society. Today's children see themselves as a sort of "social equal" with their parents, refusing to be "seen and not heard" or otherwise treated disrespectfully.*

*Note: Because *Active Parenting Today* was first published in the United States, historical references refer to this democratic society. Because each democratic society has its own story to tell, parents in countries other than the U.S. may wish to share ways in which their own struggle for equality was achieved.

Equal and Different

The concept that "all (people) are created equal" does not mean that all people are created the same. Differences between people range from the obvious, such as how we look, to the subtle, such as our dreams and values. People also have different roles they play and different responsibilities depending on those roles.

In spite of these differences, we are each considered of equal value and worth under our constitution. This means we are entitled to equal protection under the law; equal opportunity for employment; an equal right to make our opinions known; and an equal right to be treated respectfully, to name a few.

Likewise, in a family parents and children are equal in some ways and different in others. One big way that parents and children are still different is in the roles they play. The parent's role is that of a leader, while the child more often plays the role of the learner. As the leaders in the family, parents have certain rights and responsibilities that differ from their children. For example, we have the responsibility of providing food, clothing, shelter and protection for our children. We also have the right to drive, vote, use alcohol, and other privileges that are not available to children.

We also have the authority to decide many of the matters that affect the lives of our children. Since this includes how we decide to parent, let's look at the concept of authority a little closer.

The Role of Authority in a Society of Equals

Even in a society of equals, authorities still exist. The president in a corporation, the police officer on the beat and the principal in the school are examples of people who have the authority to make final decisions in their domains and the responsibility to enforce those decisions. They are the leaders. However, it's not much use being a leader if no one is willing to follow you. Here, then, is an important principle of leadership:

Leaders get their authority from those they lead.

The same is true for parents. We are the authorities in our families. But to be effective, we must have the cooperation of our children. Let's look at three types of leadership, and how effective each is likely to be in our current society.

1. Autocratic Style: The Dictator

A dictator is one who has absolute control, and the autocratic parent is all-powerful in dictating the lives of his or her children. This parent is a dominating figure who rewards and punishes to enforce his orders. Children are told what to do, how to do it and when to do it. There is little or no room for them to question, challenge or disagree. The dictator method of parenting worked reasonably well in times when inequality was normal between people, but it works poorly in today's time of equality.

Children who grow up in autocratic families seldom thrive. Either they have their spirits broken and give up, or, more often, they rebel. This rebellion usually happens during the teen years, because the child has developed enough power to fight back. The dictator has been the typical parenting style for so many generations that teenage rebellion has come to be accepted by many experts as "normal." This is a mistake. Teenagers do not have to rebel to become independent.

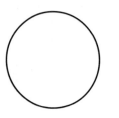

The dictator can be described as using "limits without freedom," and depicted as a closed circle.

2. Permissive Style: The Doormat

Permissive parents are those who are reacting strongly against the harsh and uncompromising autocratic method. Permissive parents allow their children to "do their own thing" too much of the time. In such households, there is little respect for order and routine, and few limits are placed on anyone's freedom. Many such parents behave like doormats, allowing their children to walk all over them. Some of these parents want to be firmer but do not know the words or discipline skills to use. One of the main drawbacks of this style is the feeling of insecurity which plagues children raised in this manner. They have almost no sense of belonging, and because they have not learned to cooperate, they are often difficult to live with.

Children with permissive parents are often pampered and accustomed to getting their own way. When someone outside the family finally tells them that rules apply to them also, these children or teens frequently rebel. It is difficult to get a child who is used to a lifestyle with no limits to voluntarily begin obeying rules.

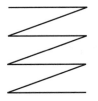

The doormat approach can be described as "freedom without limits" and shown as a squiggly line, meaning freedom run rampant.

3. Democratic Style: The Active Parent

The democratic style is, in some respects, the middle ground between the autocratic and permissive styles, but it is also much more. In an active household, freedom is an ideal, but so are the rights of others and the responsibilities of all. The parent is the leader who encourages cooperation and stimulates learning. There is order and routine, and every person is an important member of the family.

The active parent acknowledges our democratic heritage and the role of social equality among all human beings in two important ways:

1. Children are treated with dignity and respect, even when their parents discipline them.

2. Children are entitled to express their thoughts and feelings, respectfully, to their parents. In this way they are given the right to influence the decisions that affect their lives. This is consistent with life in a democratic country:

Democracy does not mean you will always get your way. It means you will always get your say.

The democratic style could be called "freedom within limits," and symbolized by a squiggly line within the limits of a circle.

In fact, it could be shown as "freedom within *expanding* limits." As the child assumes more and more responsibility, the parent gradually relaxes the limits, until eventually a teenager leaving home has the same amount of independence as you or I do.

The Fallacy of Reward and Punishment

We mentioned earlier that reward and punishment are tools the dictator parent uses to enforce his orders. Children are kept in line by the threat of punishment if they misbehave and the promise of reward if they do what the parent wishes them to do. This system of reward and punishment may have been effective in older days when the world was ruled by kings and queens and emperors and everyone "knew his place," but in a society of equals, it doesn't work very well.

A reward for good behavior comes to be expected almost as a right.

For one thing, a reward for good behavior comes to be expected almost as a right. The child does not learn to behave cooperatively just because the situation calls for it, or because the family functions better when everyone follows the rules or pitches in. Instead, he develops a "what's in it for me?" attitude that leads him to expect more and more rewards for positive behavior. The parent must then increase the value of the reward to keep it effective until she reaches a point of frustration. This frustration often leads to the use of punishment.

Punishment is not effective in the long run because it often creates resentment on the part of the child.

Punishment continues to be a popular method for many parents because it does appear to work in the short run. Under the threat of punishment, children will often improve negative behavior. However, punishment is not effective in the long run because it often creates resentment on the part of the child. In a society of equals, when you hurt someone, you give that person a sort of unspoken right to hurt you back. Children will usually find ways of getting even through future misbehavior or worse.

In fact, reward and punishment are out of place among equals. It is only a superior who can give rewards and mete out punishments, and it is only inferiors who can receive them. All in all, rewards and punishments as methods of child-raising are holdovers from an earlier time when the world was a different place. There are much more effective methods of discipline, and we will become acquainted with them in this program.

What Kind of Child Do We Want To Raise?

Since the most important purpose of families has always been the survival of their members, and the teaching of survival skills to their children, it makes sense that the kind of child we would want to raise is a child who will survive in a democratic environment. And, to be complete, we would say not only "survive" but also "thrive." So what qualities are important for surviving and thriving in a democratic society? We think there are at least four:

Courage is a foundation upon which the child constructs her personality.

- **Courage** is the first. Alfred Adler once said that if he could give one gift to a child, it would be courage. If a child were courageous, he reasoned, that child could learn everything else she needed to learn. Coupled with parental guidance, a child's courage enables the child to try, fail and try again, until she masters the challenges life poses. With too little courage, the child gives up easily or does not try at all. Fear leads to failure, and failure reinforces fear. Such a cycle of discouragement supports a lifelong attitude of regret and resentment. Courage is a foundation upon which the child constructs her personality. It is at the heart of human potential. In this course we consider courage to be so essential to the child's development that we devote much of the second chapter to methods of encouraging children, and we will be referring to courage again and again.

- **Self-esteem** is the second quality necessary for thriving in a democratic society. Simply stated, self-esteem is the opinion we have of ourselves. When a child's self-esteem is high, he sees himself as a capable human being who has a good opportunity to succeed at challenges. He also knows that even failure is nothing more than an opportunity for learning, so when he doesn't succeed at first, he does not give up either. This experience of himself as a winner gives the child the courage to tackle life's problems through positive behavior, and to take advantage of the wonderful opportunities available in a democratic society. We will explore the critical connection between self-esteem, courage and behavior in Chapter Two.

- **Responsibility** is the third quality a child needs to thrive. Democracy demands that its members make decisions and accept responsibility for

Democracy demands that its members make decisions and accept responsibility for the consequences of those decisions.

the consequences of those decisions. Without individual responsibility, our cherished freedoms will give way to governmental responsibility, where the state will make decisions for us.

With freedom and choice comes the responsibility for the consequences of those choices. The reality of our society is that its children will be called upon to makes thousands of choices, and they will be held responsible for their choices by experiencing the consequences that follow. Some of these choices will be life and death matters. They will be offered drugs; will they choose to accept? They will face choices about drinking, sex, crime, dropping out, and even suicide. And their parents won't be there to tell them what to do. But if they have been prepared to make responsible decisions, and have developed the courage to stand behind these decisions, they will be prepared to meet these challenges. We will explore methods designed to teach responsibility to children throughout the program and especially in Chapter Four.

■ **Cooperation** is the fourth essential quality children need to develop in order to thrive. In some circles a great deal of emphasis has been placed on competition as the road to success. In reality it has always been those individuals who have been aware of the magic of teamwork who have moved society forward. Helping a child learn that life is neither dependent nor independent, but rather an interdependent experience, is a cornerstone of *Active Parenting Today*. In a society of equals, cooperation skills have high value, and the child who can cooperate with others in any enterprise is far more likely to survive and thrive than one who has never learned. The relationship of child and parent is ideally one of cooperation rather than conflict. But cooperation from the child cannot be demanded; it must be won. In each session we will focus on a particular method of achieving cooperative relationships between parent and child through Family Enrichment Activities. In addition, Chapter Five is devoted to teaching ways of winning cooperation through effective communication skills.

Cooperation from the child cannot be demanded; it must be won.

The goal of this book is to provide you with the information and skills that will enable you to raise courageous, responsible and cooperative children with high self-esteem. These qualities will be discussed frequently in these chapters, and they will be woven into every aspect of the program—video presentations, class discussions, role plays, reading assignments and home activities. As you learn, we urge you to stay aware of your own responsible, cooperative and courageous behavior, and to reinforce your own self-esteem.

The Method of Choice

One of the single most powerful forces in existence is that of human choice. So powerful is this concept that nations will go to war to preserve their right to choose how to live their lives. When we say that the hallmark of the active style of parenting is "freedom within limits," what we are really talking about is the freedom of the child to make choices.

Just as a people will rise up and overthrow a dictator, a child will resist a parent who robs her of a chance to share in the decisions that affect her life. The parent who is neither a dictator nor a doormat, but is an active leader in the family will use this knowledge to handle problems and teach responsibility.

The freedom to choose is tremendously empowering to children.

Choice is power. As leader in the family, you can give your child choices that are appropriate for his age and level of responsibility. This, again, is the idea of freedom within expanding limits. The freedom to choose is tremendously empowering to children. And because you limit what choices the child is allowed to make, family rules and values are not sacrificed.

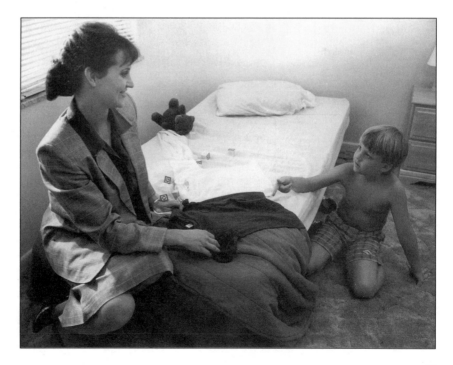

Don't Boss. Give a Choice.

Even young children can be given simple choices. Allowing your child the opportunity to practice decision making can become a regular part of your daily routine. This can also be useful in helping resolve conflicts as we saw on the video in the example between Laura and Zack. After unsuccessfully trying to coerce Zack into wearing his white shirt, Laura gives Zack a choice.

Laura: *"Would you rather wear this white shirt or the blue one?"*

This gives Zack some power over the decisions that affect his life, so he has less need to rebel. Of course, he chooses the blue one, which is acceptable to Laura. Had he chosen a shirt that was unacceptable for the situation, Laura would have limited his choice.

Laura: *"I'm sorry, Zack, the T-shirt with spaghetti stains just isn't appropriate for going out. How about the yellow shirt?"*

As children get older, the choices they are given can become more open-ended. So instead of either the blue or white shirt, you might simply ask the child what he would like to wear. The following are some examples of choices you can use.

Give Children Choices

Age 1-5	Age 6-12
"Would you like orange juice or grapefruit juice this morning?"	"Would you like to help me do the grocery shopping and help choose what we buy?"
"Can you put this away yourself, or would you like some help?"	"Do you prefer to set homework time for before dinner or afterwards?"
"Would you like to pick out a book or would you like me to choose a book for your bedtime story?"	"Would you rather go visit Grandma on Saturday or Sunday?"
"Would you like to take your bath now or after one more song?"	"Which chores would you like to do?"

A word of caution: Don't get carried away and make everything a choice. Sometimes children want and need a firm but friendly decision from a parent.

Family Enrichment Activity

Taking Time for Fun

Ever notice that a good salesperson will always spend time developing a positive relationship with you before she tries to sell you anything? She knows that half the job of effectively influencing a person is first developing that relationship. Once the person has been "won over," the sale is much easier. (Can you imagine a salesperson being autocratic and demanding a sale? "You'll buy this because I'm the salesperson and I said so!")

The more you can enrich your relationship with your child, the more he will allow you to be an influence in his life.

The same is true for parenting. The more you can enrich your relationship with your child, the more he will allow you to be an influence in his life. This will prevent many problems as well as make discipline much easier when it is called for.

We will present a Family Enrichment Activity in each chapter. Use these, and the other support skills, to strengthen your relationship. If your child is frequently out of control, this may be a way to begin making positive contact. Be creative. Reach out.

The first family enrichment activity is to take time to do something fun with your child. It can be as brief as a few minutes, or as long as a day. The key is to make it fun and to try making it a regular part of your relationship. In other words, "Every day a little play." For example:

- Throw a ball or shoot baskets.
- Bake a special dessert.
- Play a game together.
- Roughhouse.
- Go on an outing . . . just the two of you.
- Tickle each other.
- Tell a joke or funny story.

To get the most out of this activity:

- Find activities you both enjoy (that have little or no cost).
- Ask for suggestions from your child, but have some ideas of your own.
- Keep it fun! Do not use this time for confrontation.
- Record your experiences in your *Parent's Guide*.

Family Enrichment Activity
Taking Time For Fun

Remember when . . .
Remember something fun you enjoyed doing as a child with one of your parents. Close your eyes for a moment and visualize the pleasant experience.

What was the fun activity you and your parent shared? _____

_____

How did you feel about your parent at that moment? _____

_____

How did you feel about yourself? _____

_____

Progress Chart
As you take time for fun with each of your children, record the experience below:

Child's name _____

What did you do? _____

_____

How did it go? _____

_____

Child's name _____

What did you do? _____

_____

How did it go? _____

_____

_____

The Method of Choice Activity

Choices I can give my child this week:

Child's name _____

Choice _____

How did it go? _____

_____

_____

Child's name _____

Choice _____

How did it go? _____

_____

_____

Child's name _____

Choice _____

How did it go? _____

_____

_____

Chapter One. Home Activities Checklist

(Check when completed.)

❑ 1. Read Chapter One. If you wish to read ahead, please do so.

❑ 2. Do the Family Enrichment Activity: Taking Time for Fun on page 23.

❑ 3. Practice giving choices to your children this week and complete the Method of Choice activity on page 24.

❑ 4. Call your buddy (optional).

Notes

Instilling Courage and Self-Esteem

A long time ago, before the advent of convenience stores, there was a group of humans called "milkmen." There was also a 5-year-old boy who was afraid of the dark. His mother, hoping to help him overcome his fear, encouraged the little boy to open the front door and bring in the milk. He was too afraid, but she persisted. "Go ahead," she said. "God is outside and He will protect you." The boy thought about that for a moment, then moved his tiny hand toward the door. He fearfully turned the knob to open the door, reached his little hand into that cold, black morning, and shouted, "If you're out there, God, hand me the milk!"

Courage . . . One From the Heart

Preparing a child to courageously meet the challenges life will certainly offer is perhaps the single most important aspect of *Active Parenting Today*. Courage is such an important quality in today's complex world of choices that it forms the very foundation upon which the child constructs her personality. From the French word "coeur," meaning "heart," courage is the "heart" that enables us to take risks. And it is through risk taking that we are able to develop responsibility, cooperation, independence . . . and whatever else we may strive for. In fact, we define courage in *Active Parenting Today* as:

The confidence to take a known risk for a known purpose.

Courage is a feeling. It is a feeling of confidence that allows us to take those risks. It is not the absence of fear but the willingness to take a reasonable risk in spite of our fear. Without this feeling of courage, we often find ourselves sitting on the sidelines, unwilling to take the risks inherent in any endeavor. Without courage, we let life pass us by while we wishfully wait for someone else to "hand us the milk."

Self-Esteem . . . One From the Mind

Where does courage come from? It comes from a belief in ourselves. A belief that we are capable, lovable human beings who will eventually succeed. This belief in ourselves is commonly called "self-esteem." In other words we hold ourselves in high regard. When we think well of ourselves, when we think we have a good chance to succeed, then it makes sense that we will have the courage to take risks.

High Self-Esteem ———⟶ Courage

Unfortunately, the opposite is also true. When we think poorly of ourselves, when we think we are not okay, that we are unlovable, not capable, then our self-esteem drops. This low self-esteem produces discouragement and fear.

Low Self-Esteem ———⟶ Discouragement

And when people of any age become discouraged, two things often happen: 1) They stop taking reasonable risks, so they stop improving; and 2) They become more likely to misbehave. We'll explore this connection between discouragement and misbehavior more in a moment, but first let's put all this together in a model for understanding human behavior.

The Think-Feel-Do Cycle

We have talked about the problems and opportunities that life poses. Let's call these "events." In other words, something happens. For example, in the video Sara froze when it was her turn to cross the log over the creek. Her family had all crossed the log, but she was afraid.

```
┌─────────────────────┐
│       EVENT         │
│  (crossing the log) │
└─────────────────────┘
```

How do we respond to events in our lives? With events that are important to us, we experience feelings. For example, Sara felt afraid to cross the log. Here's where many people share a common misconception. They talk as if the events in their lives cause their feelings. For example, they might say that crossing the log made Sara afraid.

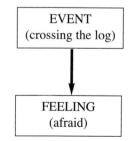

This is a mistake. Although other people and events do influence or trigger our feelings, the cause of our feelings is our thinking. As the Greek philosopher Epictetus said:

"Men are not disturbed by things, but by the view they take of things."

So it isn't crossing the log that caused Sara's feelings of fear in our example, but rather her thoughts about falling off the log—her "view" of the situation. What kind of thoughts might generate a feeling of fear? There are many possibilities.

"I'm not good at things."
"I might hurt myself or get wet."
"My parents won't like me anymore."

Whatever the exact beliefs, we can notice the strong feeling of fear Sara is expressing, and guess that she is thinking negatively about herself. These thoughts lower her self-esteem, which makes her feel discouraged.

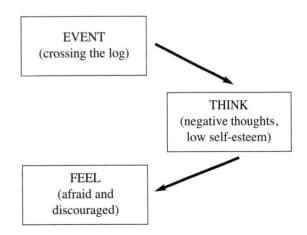

To complete our cycle, we add one final part: our behavior, what we *do* in response to an event. As you can probably guess from the model, what we *do* is a result of what we think and how we feel. When self-esteem is high and the child feels a strong sense of courage, behavior is going to be positive. But when negative thinking leads to low self-esteem and discouragement, behavior is likely to be negative.

What we *do* is particularly important because this is how we influence (notice we say "influence," not "control") the events in our lives. In the case of Sara, she eventually chose to give in to her fear and run home. This becomes a failure that may lower her opinion of herself even more, leading to further discouragement and other negative behavior. This can be compounded if her family offers critical and discouraging comments when she gives up. The result is often a failure cycle.

Failure Cycle

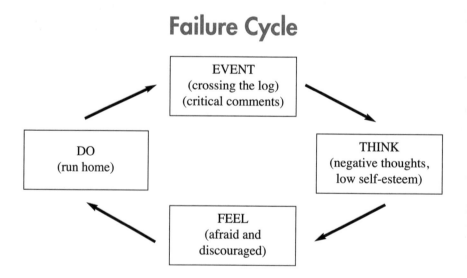

But let's say that Sara had high self-esteem and had been taught how to think positively about challenges. Then her thinking might be:

"I know that I'm afraid, but sometimes it's good to do things even though you're afraid."

"This isn't really very high, and if I fall I won't get hurt, just wet. And that's not so terrible."

"Anyway, I'm pretty good at crossing things, like the balance beam on the playground at school."

"And if I do fail, I can handle that, too. After all, failing at something doesn't make a person a failure. It just means they need some more practice."

With thinking like this, she may feel afraid but certainly not frozen or discouraged. Her positive thoughts have kept her self-esteem high and given her the courage to risk continuing the effort. Her attitude about learning will probably create positive events in the future. She is operating in a success cycle.

Success Cycle

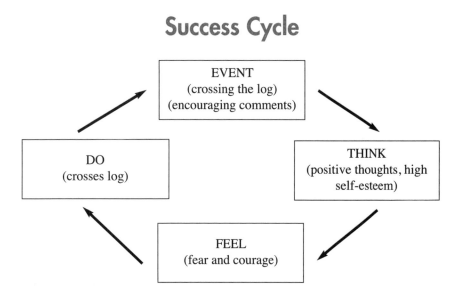

EVENT
(crossing the log)
(encouraging comments)

THINK
(positive thoughts, high self-esteem)

FEEL
(fear and courage)

DO
(crosses log)

What Can Parents Do?

Helping our children get into success cycles and stay there is a goal for all parents. It is therefore important for us to become skilled at encouraging the development of self-esteem and courage. But what does that word "encouraging" really mean?

Breaking the word into two parts, "en-courage" means to "instill courage." Rudolf Dreikurs once said that "children need encouragement like plants need water." The remainder of this chapter will help you strengthen your skills in this critical area of parenting.

Encouragement: "Catch 'em Doing Good"

Imagine yourself in this situation: You are driving your car from work or from shopping. Suddenly, in your rearview mirror you see a police car with blue lights flashing, and it is following you. Anxiously, you pull over, wondering what you did wrong. You notice your rapid heartbeat, the perspiration forming on your palms, your dry mouth. The policeman approaches your car window and asks for your driver's license. He looks at the license, then at you, and says, "You know, I've been on the force for 12 years, and it's always a pleasure to see a courteous driver. I pulled you over so I could congratulate you on the fine driving skill you showed back there in that traffic tangle at the freeway overpass. If every driver was as courteous and considerate as you were, we could avoid lots of snarls and headaches. So I just wanted to say, 'Thanks.'"

What do you think your reactions would be to the policeman's comment?

    a. You would feel good about yourself; you'd be a little proud.
    b. You would feel that you are a pretty good driver.
    c. You would feel encouraged to drive more courteously and
       considerately in the future.
    d. You'd almost faint from the shock!

The chances are response "d" was your strongest. We just do not expect to receive such compliments from authority figures. And yet, in the above example, after the shock has worn off and you are driving away, you probably would feel good about yourself, think that you are a pretty good driver, and feel encouraged to drive more courteously and considerately in the future.

This is because the policeman's comment was an example of the power of encouragement. With only a few words, he increased your self-esteem, gave a boost to your confidence, and created the likelihood that you would drive even better in the future. No wonder we call encouragement "the subtle giant."

Before we look further at encouragement, let's consider its opposite—discouragement—and the ways it affects children's behavior.

Avoid Discouraging

The misbehaving child is usually a "dis-couraged" child.

The misbehaving child is usually a *dis-couraged* child. Somewhere along the line, he has lost the courage to face life's problems with positive behavior. Instead, such children have come to believe that the only path open to them is the easier, negative approach.

In order to build children's self-esteem and courage, we want to first become aware of some common ways we may be discouraging them. Remembering the think-feel-do cycle, if we become discouraging events in our children's lives, we tend to lower their self-esteem, which leads to dis-couragement, which leads to negative behavior . . . which may prompt us to become even more punishing and discouraging. To change this cycle, see which, if any, of these common discouraging influences you need to avoid:

To build children's self-esteem and courage, we want to first become aware of some common ways we may be discouraging them.

- **Negative Expectations.** If people who are important to you don't believe in your ability, you probably won't believe in it either. They don't have to say so; you can usually tell what they think of you by the way they act around you and the words they use with you. You pick up on those things pretty easily. Of course, sometimes they make their opinions of you pretty clear by saying such things as:

"No, you can't use that! You'll break it."

"I guess you're just not the type who does well in school."

- **Focusing on Mistakes.** If somebody who is important to you spends a lot of time telling you what you do wrong, you come to believe there is more wrong with you than right. It becomes harder to do things right because you are paying so much attention to your mistakes and blunders.

"I notice you left your glass in the den again last night. How many times do I have to ask you to be more considerate?"

"This doesn't look good where you colored outside the lines, does it?"

- **Perfectionism** (expecting too much). If your parents expect more from you than you are able to give, then you gradually stop trying, because you know you will never be able to satisfy them. You may decide to make your mark in other ways, like misbehaving. Since you can't be the best at being the best, maybe you will set your goal at being the best at being the worst.

"How did you misspell 'circus' when you got all the others right? If you'd really thought about it, you would have had a perfect paper."

"This isn't a bad report card. But with your potential, you could have done better."

■ **Overprotection** (expecting too little). If somebody who is important to you spends too much time telling you how dangerous and difficult the world is, you may come to believe that you can't handle things for yourself. You may let them handle things for you. If you get in trouble at school or with the law, they are there to bail you out. And if you never experience the consequences of your mistakes, you could begin to get the idea that you can do anything you like. But strangely you find yourself not feeling very confident, though you may act over-confident to make up for it.

"Sure, I'll be glad to go down to the school and talk to your teacher. I'm sure when she realizes how hard you worked, she'll change your grade."

"No, you can't ride the bus with the other kids. I'll feel better if I drive you myself."

Turning Discouragement Into Encouragement

You have just read four main ways that parents (and teachers) often discourage children. Fortunately, these dis-couragers can be turned around to become ways of en-couraging our children:

How To Discourage	How To Encourage
1. Have negative expectations	1. Show confidence
2. Focus on mistakes	2. Build on strengths
3. Perfectionism (expecting too much)	3. Value the child
4. Overprotection (expecting too little)	4. Stimulate independence

Let's look more closely at these ways of encouraging, which, by the way, are also effective in work situations and other adult-adult relationships:

1. How To Show Confidence

A cornerstone of self-esteem and courage is the belief that we are capable. As we achieve success in solving life's problems and learning new skills, our belief in ourselves grows. But tackling problems and attempting new skills takes confidence. Parents can help by showing this confidence in their children. Here are some ways to do this:

Give responsibilities in line with what you know about your child's abilities.

■ **Give responsibility.** Giving your child responsibility is a nonverbal way of showing confidence. It is a way of saying, "I know you can do this." Of course, you want to give responsibilities in line with what you know about your child's abilities, or the standards may be set too high. Here are some examples of giving responsibility in ways that demonstrate confidence:

"I will agree to your keeping the dog, Julie, if you will accept the responsibility of feeding and caring for her."

"I think you have handled getting yourself up in the morning really well, so you can probably handle staying up later now—say, 9:00 p.m. What do you think?"

■ **Ask your child's opinion or advice.** Children like to have parents lean on their knowledge or judgment. When you ask your child's opinion, you are demonstrating confidence in his ability to make a useful contribution. If you ask your child to teach you something, it shows confidence in his knowledge and skills. Asking for his opinions in such ways helps bolster his self-esteem:

"Which route do you think would be best on our trip to visit Grandma and Grandpa?"

"What would you like to do with the toys that get left on the floor?"

"Would you teach me how to play the new game?"

"Well, what were the reasons for the Civil War?"

It is an act of confidence in our children's abilities when we refuse to step in and take over when they become discouraged.

■ **Avoid the temptation to take over.** It is an act of confidence in our children's abilities when we refuse to step in and take over when they become discouraged. What a temptation it is, this tendency to relieve their discomfort by doing the thing that is so hard for them and so easy for us! But when we give in to the temptation, we are not showing confidence in the child. If we do something for the child on a regular basis that she, with a little persistence, could do independently, then we are communicating that we do not have confidence in her ability to follow a task through to the end. When we bail her out of the consequences of misbehavior, we rob her of an important lesson in responsibility. We say in effect that we don't have confidence in her ability to handle the consequences of her actions.

All in all, taking over is not a way to encourage children who are discouraged, it is a way to certify their discouragement. Such children often show an inability to tolerate frustration. When things don't work out immediately, they give up—often having a "frustration tantrum."

"Keep trying, you can do it!"

"No, I can't stop the kids from picking on you. But I can talk to you about some things that you can do."

2. How To Build on the Child's Strengths

I learned an important lesson as a young counselor: "If you want a child to do better, find something about the child that you like." Focusing our attention on what's right with our children, rather than what is wrong, is tremendously

Focusing our attention on what's right with our children, rather than what is wrong, is tremendously encouraging.

encouraging. And, as we've seen, encouragement leads to improved self-esteem, which leads to courage and positive behavior . . . in other words, a success cycle.

The key is to break the learning down into small steps. Remember, you didn't learn the alphabet all at once. You learned "A," then "B," then "C," all the way to "Z." This A to Z process is the same for anything from teaching specific skills to character traits. Whether it is helping a child learn to complete his homework, or teaching him to be honest, we can systematically build on strengths to accomplish this.

■ **Acknowledge what your child does well.** Once you know where you would like the child to end up (for example, having good study habits or being an honest individual), get an idea where the child is on the A to Z path towards reaching that goal. It is unlikely that he can't read a word or answers every question with a lie; he will be somewhere between A and Z. Now you have a place to start. Acknowledge what he can do.

The key is to break the learning down into small steps.

"This is terrific! You've completed two assignments. This is the way to get ahead at school. I can really see that you've worked hard at this, but then I know you can work hard . . . I've seen you on the basketball court."

"I'm not thrilled that you borrowed my hammer without asking, but I do appreciate your owning up to it when I asked. I appreciate the honesty."

It is much more effective to "catch 'em doing good" than our traditional approach of catching them doing bad. In addition to acknowledging their progress on the A to Z course, it also helps to acknowledge other areas where the child is already experiencing some success. This helps build the self-esteem that translates into risk taking and other successes. The parent who brought in the basketball connection in the previous example was using this strength-building technique effectively.

Examples like the following offer children a healthy diet of encouragement:

"It was really a pleasure having you out to dinner with us tonight. Your manners were great. Let's do it again soon."

"Thank you for helping with the dishes."

"I appreciate your playing quietly while I took a nap. That was very considerate."

"It sure is fun to play with you when you take turns with me."

- **Encourage taking the next step.** Children get a sense of self-esteem from learning, whether it be a sport, a school subject, or a skill. Learning, however, requires many steps (A to Z) and much improvement. It also requires risk, because with each new step, there is the potential for failure. Even with children who have strong self-esteem, there are times when their fear of failure paralyzes them, making it difficult for them to take the next step. And there are times for all of us when the frustration of not progressing the way we'd like undermines our courage and tempts us to give up. This is when an encouraging word from a parent or teacher can help give the child enough courage to take the risk. For example:

"Learning to do division can be frustrating, and I guess you feel like giving up. But if you'll just stick with it, I know you'll get it. Look how far you've come already! Now, how about tackling that last problem again?"

"I know it hasn't been easy, but you've really improved in being honest with us. And we're feeling like we can trust you more. So, if you still want to spend the night at Carrie's house, it's okay with us."

- **Concentrate on improvement, not perfection.** The mistake most people make in the encouragement process is to wait until the child attains the desired result (Z on the A to Z path) before offering praise or encouragement. The key to encouragement, however, is to break the process down into a lot of small steps, offering encouragement along the entire route. Any improvement, no matter how small, is a step in the right direction and should be noticed. Since success is a great motivator, we want the child to be able to experience numerous successes along the way. This builds self-esteem and keeps the child moving towards the goal. If the child falls back a step, and that's to be expected, she needs our encouragement to keep at it and not give up. In fact, her effort alone, even when she's not making progress, can still be encouraged.

In fact, her effort alone, even when she's not making progress, can still be encouraged.

"Great! You are really getting good at writing down all of your assignments. One more day and you'll have a whole week."

"Thanks for telling us about not turning in your homework on Monday. That took a lot of courage. We'll talk about what to do about it in a minute, but first I want you to know how much we admire your efforts to be more honest."

"I can really see the effort that went into this."

"Hey, this room is really looking good. You've gotten all your books picked up, and the bed's even made. If you like, I have some time and could help you figure out a system for organizing your closet."

3. How To Value the Child

A child's self-esteem does not spring from achievements alone. Much more important for most people is that they are accepted by significant people in their lives—that they belong. In fact, much success hunting is really aimed at trying to win the acceptance of those significant people. Ironically, what most of us really want deep down inside is to be accepted for ourselves, not just for our achievements. This is what it means to feel a sense of belonging.

Children who feel accepted by their parents have a tremendous bedrock of self-esteem upon which to construct a healthy, happy life.

Children who feel accepted by their parents have a tremendous bedrock of self-esteem upon which to construct a healthy, happy life. Without it, some of the richest, most successful people in history have lived lives of quiet desperation, wondering why their successes were never satisfying.

The goal is to communicate to our children that win or lose, pass or fail, in trouble or out of trouble, we are still their parents *and we are glad of it.* We all need this unconditional acceptance from someone, and if we don't get it from our parents, then we need to get it someplace else: from a substitute parent, or even a therapist. For some, a belief in God fulfills this same human need for unconditional acceptance.

■ **Separate worth from accomplishments.** A child's worth is less a matter of what he does, and more a matter of who he is. You can let your child know that while you admire his successes and share his disappointment in his failures, you love him for himself. You can put emphasis on the activities themselves and not just on the results. You can encourage your child while he is doing a task instead of waiting until the task is completed.

"I'm glad you enjoy learning."

"Playing your hardest is more important than winning."

"Losing doesn't make a person a loser."

There are no bad children, only bad behavior.

■ **Separate worth from misbehavior.** Just as a child's worth is something different from the sum total of her accomplishments, so is it different from her mistakes or failures. There are no bad children, only bad behavior. If a child is labeled "bad," or "no good," she may eventually come to believe that the label is true. When this happens, bad behavior then becomes appropriate. After all, what should we expect from "bad" people but "bad" behavior? For this reason, it is important that we refrain from labeling children and avoid shaming them for their mistakes or misbehavior. Children who grow up "ashamed of themselves" have a difficult time regaining their lost self-esteem and courage.

Mistakes, like misbehavior, are not indications of a lack of worth, but are actually part of growth and development. A mistake can teach a valuable lesson, showing a child what not to do in the future. We want to help children, especially perfectionistic children, learn to make friends with their mistakes. Mistakes, as we have said, are tools for learning.

Help them accept mistakes with a smile rather than a kick.

Children (and adults) who are afraid of being imperfect actually retard their own growth and development. A perfectionist, according to one joke, is a person who won't attempt a foreign language until he can speak it fluently. As this quip implies, a fear of mistakes yields a fear of trying, which in turn yields less learning. Since one of our goals is to help children learn, we want to help them accept mistakes with a smile rather than a kick.

"No, you're not bad, but it is bad to put crayon on the walls."

"When we get angry at you, it doesn't mean we don't like you. It means we don't like something you've done."

"Mistakes are for learning. When we make a mistake, we don't blame. We correct it."

"I guess you made a mistake. Well, let's see what you can learn from it."

■ **Appreciate the child's uniqueness.** Although it is important to teach children that all people are equal, that doesn't mean all people are the same. It is encouraging for your child to know that he is unique, special, one of a kind. You can appreciate your child's uniqueness by taking an interest in his activities. Most of all, you can say and do things that show your child you love him for his unique self, and for no other reason.

"Anyway, that's my opinion, what's yours?"

"When I see you from a distance, I can tell it's you from your walk."

"This room is really you! I could never have decorated it for you."

"You are the only you in the whole world. What luck that you happen to be my daughter!"

"I love you."

4. How To Stimulate Independence

Independence, or the ability to stand on one's own two feet, is essential for thriving in our democratic society. In fact, when we keep our children overly dependent on us, we pay a price; as psychologist Haim Ginott once wrote, "Dependence breeds hostility." The last thing we want to do as parents is to keep our children overly dependent on us. (Remember, one goal of parenting is to work ourselves out of a job.)

As we encourage our children towards independence, we also want to keep in mind that they will benefit enormously by learning to cooperate, as we mentioned in Chapter One. "No man is an island" expresses the truth that interdependence—independent individuals choosing to work together cooperatively—offers the best chance for success of both the individual and the human community.

Independence, or the ability to stand on one's own two feet, is essential for thriving in our democratic society.

■ **Avoid pampering your child.** When parents put themselves into the child's service or otherwise treat the child like a privileged character, the child eventually becomes dependent, spoiled and discouraged. Some signs of pampering a child over the age of seven include: calling her more than once to get up in the morning; routinely driving the child places on short notice; picking out her clothes; giving her money on demand instead of an allowance; allowing the child to curse at you or otherwise speak disrespectfully (this should not be allowed at any age); making your child's homework your responsibility; allowing her to eat meals in front of the TV; cleaning up after her; not requiring her to help with family chores; and rescuing her from the consequences of her misbehavior.

You can let your child know that you have decided to stop pampering her.

If you find some of these examples hitting home, then you can let your child know that you have decided to stop pampering her, and begin treating her more respectfully. You can do this in a firm yet friendly way, taking responsibility yourself, while even encouraging the child. For example:

"I want to apologize for treating you like you didn't have the good sense to handle ___ (e.g., getting yourself up in the morning; your own money; your own homework; picking up your own clothes). From now on I'm going to stop treating you like a baby and leave that up to you."

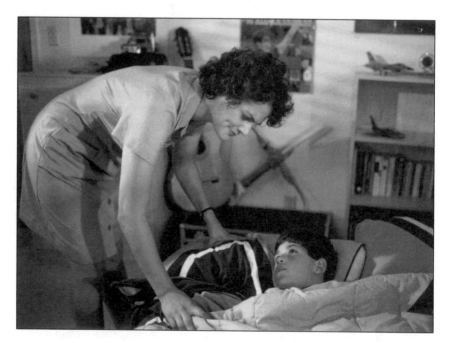

"I don't use that kind of language when I'm angry with you; I don't expect you to use it when you are angry with me."

"I'll be glad to show you where dirty clothes go, but from now on I'm only washing the clothes that get put there."

■ **Help the child develop a sense of interdependence.** Because belonging is a basic goal of all humans, it deserves special emphasis. You can invite cooperative behavior on the part of your child, with the aim of letting him experience the pleasure and benefits of group efforts.

"You're an important part of this family, and we'd like your ideas at family council meetings." (More on "The Family Council Meeting" in Chapter Six.)

"Why don't you come up on the sofa and snuggle with us?"

"Would you like to make lasagna with us?"

Family Enrichment Activity

Letter of Encouragement

As a young Sunday School teacher, I became annoyed with the idea of having to give grades to my students. Grades seemed an inadequate way to express either their progress or the way I felt about them after sharing nine months together. I decided to write each of my students a personal letter to go with the grades. While writing the letters, I found myself describing the positive aspects of each child and how he or she was progressing. These "letters of encouragement" were received appreciatively as the children left for summer vacation.

I didn't think much more about the letters until four years later. I was at a reception when a woman approached me and introduced herself as the mother of one of my students from that same Sunday School class. "That letter you wrote Alice meant so much to her," she said. "You know she still has it on her bulletin board."

All of the encouragement skills discussed in this session could be considered as family enrichment activities. But somehow "putting it in writing" carries extra weight in our society. In addition, the child can refer back to a letter of encouragement in the future and rekindle the warm feeling it generated, just as Alice did. This week's activity is to write a letter of encouragement to each of your children. Let your letter have the following characteristics:

- Write about your child's improvement in some area, not necessarily perfection.

- Write only truthful statements; don't say that the child has improved when he really hasn't.

- Be specific about what the improvements are.

- Write how the child's behavior has been helpful to others.

A parent's letter might look like this:

Dear Megan,

Your mother and I have been noticing how well you are doing with your reading. We can really hear the improvement. All that practice has really begun to pay off!

I also noticed something last weekend when we were visiting Grandma and Grandpa that made me feel very good inside. It was when you were playing with your little brother outside. You were so gentle and kind to him. You made sure he was okay, and you made sure to let him take turns holding the rocks that you found. I thought about how lucky he is to have a sister like you. In fact, how lucky you are to have each other.

Anyway, I just wanted you to know how much I am enjoying watching you grow, and how glad I am that you are my daughter.
Love,
Daddy

Family Enrichment Activity
Letter of Encouragement

Remember when . . .
Recall a time when one of your parents said or did something that you found encouraging when you were a child. Take a moment to visualize the experience and to rekindle the positive feeling it provided.

What did your parent do or say? _____

_____

How did you feel? _____

_____

Now, try to find a letter or note that you found encouraging . . . from your parents or someone else.

What encouraged you about it? _____

_____

Use this space to write a rough draft of a letter of encouragement to each of your children. Then copy the letter onto stationery or other paper before placing it where your child will find it—or mailing it!

_____

_____

_____

_____

_____

_____

_____

_____

_____

_____

_____

Encouragement Video Practice

Discouraging and encouraging events* →→→	Put yourself in the child's place; what would you probably . . .		
	THINK →→→	FEEL →→→	DO
Scene 1 (Ben and the cereal.)			
Scene 2 (Ben and the cereal.)			
Scene 3 (Janelle and her homework.)			
Scene 4 (Janelle and her homework.)			

*Discouraging Influences

- Negative expectations
- Focusing on mistakes
- Perfectionism (expecting too much)
- Overprotection (expecting too little)

*Encouraging Influences

- Showing confidence
- Building on strengths
- Valuing the child
- Stimulating independence

Building on Strengths Activity

We all have abilities and qualities that enable us to survive and to thrive in our democratic society. Think about them in your family, filling in the names of your children (and spouse if you are married) as you go.

BELONGING

One thing that others like about me is _____

_____

One thing I like about _____ is _____

One thing I like about _____ is _____

LEARNING

One thing that I am learning is _____

One thing that _____ is learning is _____

One thing that _____ is learning is _____

CONTRIBUTING

One way I contribute to my family is _____

_____

One way that _____ contributes to our family is _____

One way that _____ contributes to our family is _____

OTHER

One other strength that I have is _____

One other strength that _____ has is _____

One other strength that _____ has is _____

Encouragement Chart

Practice using encouraging statements this week. To help you stay aware of your own efforts to be more encouraging, use the chart below to record your encouraging statements.

Child's Name   Day   Encouraging Statements

Stimulating Independence

Think of things that you are now doing for your children that they could be doing for themselves. For example, making their beds, picking up their clothes, cleaning up after them, etc. Make a list below:

1. _____

2. _____

3. _____

4. _____

5. _____

6. _____

7. _____

8. _____

Now, choose one of these to let each child do for him or herself this week. Be sure to be encouraging as you turn this over to each child, and practice your encouragement skills as each child progresses.

Afterwards . . .

What did you like about how it went? _____

_____

_____

_____

What can you do to improve things next time? _____

_____

_____

_____

Chapter Two. Home Activities Checklist

(Check when completed.)

❏ 1. Read Chapter Two. If you wish to read ahead, please do so.

❏ 2. Write each child a letter of encouragement and complete guide sheet on page 46.

❏ 3. Practice making encouraging statements and record your progress on the chart on page 49.

❏ 4. Complete the Stimulating Independence activity on page 50.

❏ 5. Continue "everyday a little play" and giving choices (from Chapter One).

❏ 6. Call your buddy (optional).

Understanding
Your Child

There is a story about a mother who had twins. One of the children was outgoing and happy and always saw the bright side of life. The other, introverted and sad, always saw the negative. The mother did not understand her two children and so took them to see a child psychologist. After the initial visit, the psychologist proposed an experiment to see how far the differences between the children went. He put the pessimistic, sad child in a room filled with dozens of exciting toys. The other child, optimistic and happy, was put in a room knee deep in horse manure. After 30 minutes, the psychologist went into the first room and found the little pessimist crying amidst his toys. "But I wanted a scooter and there aren't any!" He then went into the second room where the little optimist was busily digging through the manure. He seemed excited and joyful, which baffled the psychologist. "Why are you so happy?" asked the psychologist. "Well," replied the little optimist, "with all this manure there just has to be a pony in here someplace, and I'm going to find it!"

Understanding children is often frustrating. When you were a child, did your parents ever indicate their frustration with you by saying such things as:

"I just don't understand you!"

"Why do you do things like that?"

"Where have I failed?"

If your parents did make comments like this, they were expressing their difficulty in understanding your behavior. The purpose of this section is to help you develop an understanding of how and why your own children behave as they do. In later sections, we will build on this understanding as you learn specific methods of actively influencing your child's development.

How Children Develop

A newborn baby is small and helpless, and absolutely dependent on someone else for her own survival. Someone else must feed, clothe, cuddle and comfort the infant. She cannot survive alone. How does such a helpless creature develop into an independent adult with a healthy lifestyle and a personality of her own? There have been many theories about this, but these two are most well-known:

- **The heredity theory**. Some experts believe that hereditary factors, transmitted from parents to children through genes and chromosomes, play a major role in forming the child's personality. With this view one could conclude that a child's development is decided by the biological package with which he or she is born. This theory says that physical, mental and emotional factors existing at birth mold the personality into its unique shape.

- **The environment theory**. Other experts believe that such influences as the child's home, surrounding neighborhood, parents, nurturing and other experiences play the dominant role in shaping the personality. With this view, one could conclude that the child is like a lump of clay, whose development is shaped by outside influences and his unique personality is the result.

It is not what we have that is important, but what we do with what we have.

But there is another school of thought which holds that while heredity and environment are important influences on personality, it is the way the child responds to or uses these influences that determines the personality. In this view, the person is not passive but active. The child is not a victim of heredity or circumstance but is self-determining and creative, building a unique personality, whether he realizes it or not, by the way he responds—by the

choices he makes—to whatever influences come along. The child's destiny is not left up to fate, but is a matter of choice. We are each responsible for who we are and what we do. It is not what we have that is important, but what we do with what we have. History is filled with examples of individuals who overcame difficult handicaps to lead satisfying lives and become contributing members of their communities.

This does not mean that heredity and environment do not *influence* our personality and behavior. These influences are the "building blocks" that individuals use to shape their lives. Since better "building blocks" will more likely result in a successful person, it is useful to consider these influences more closely. Some of these building blocks are heredity, family atmosphere, family constellation and methods of parenting.

A Look at the "Building Blocks" of Personality

■ **Heredity.** The biological package the child inherits from her parents is an important resource the child uses to build a personality. For example, suppose that the child is taller than others of the same age. The child could respond to that biological fact in many ways—by being proud of her height; by feeling awkward about it; by standing tall; by stooping; by trying to dominate smaller playmates; by showing them that she will not try to dominate them; by feeling physically uncoordinated; or by excelling at basketball. The way the child responds to height, appearance, or any other physical characteristics, whether it be an asset or a handicap, is one of the many ways the child shapes her own personality.

The kind of atmosphere that exists in the family's home is very important.

■ **Family Atmosphere.** For the young child, the family is the world. Almost all of the child's early influences come from the family. The kind of atmosphere that exists in the family's home is therefore very important. What does it feel like to live in the home? Is there a feeling of mutual respect and cooperation? Are family members' rights respected? Are the parents warm and caring? Is there good humor? Is there time for fun? Are girls "sugar and spice" and boys "rotten, made of cotton"? Whatever atmosphere prevails, the child will respond to it, and the responses could take many forms: optimism, pessimism, cheerfulness, shyness, curiosity, rebelliousness, and on and on. The possible responses to the day-to-day atmosphere in the family world are endless, and the child uses them as building blocks in the construction of his personality.

■ **Family Constellation.** Another influence on your child is the number of other children in the family and the order of birth. No two children come into exactly the same family. For example, a firstborn child comes into a family

consisting of two adults (sometimes only one adult). The second child enters a family made up of adults *and* a child. The child's position in the family influences the role she chooses to play in that family and in the world in general. There are some typical responses most first children, or most youngest children, or most middle children have to their situations. There is a chart on the next page showing some of those responses. They illustrate yet another way in which children—by using the building block of the family constellation—choose to form their personalities. The chart also shows some ways in which parents can avoid magnifying the negative aspects of these characteristics.

In using the chart, keep in mind that when more than five years exist between any two children, the effect is as if there were two separate families. For example:

Lisa (16) treated as if an "only" child
Jason (9) treated as if a "first" child
Susan (7) treated as if a "second" child

Family Constellation Chart

POSITION	TYPICAL CHARACTERISTICS	TIPS FOR PARENTS
First Child	• Often takes responsibility for other siblings. • Gets along well with authority figures. • Likely to become a high achiever. • Needs to feel right, perfect, superior.	• Avoid pressure to succeed. • Encourage the fun of participating, not the goal of winning. • Teach that "mistakes are for learning." • Show "how to be gentle with yourself" when accepting failure.
Only Child	• Used to being the center of attention. • Unsure of self in many ways. • May feel incompetent compared to others (e.g., parents). • Likely to be responsible. • Often refuses to cooperate if fails to get own way.	• Provide learning opportunities with other children. • Encourage visiting friends. • Have spend-the-night company. • Utilize childcare and nursery schools.
Second Child	• May try to catch up with older child's competence. • May try to be older child's opposite in many ways. • May rebel in order to find own place.	• Encourage child's uniqueness. • Avoid comparisons with oldest. • Allow second child to handle his own conflicts with the oldest.
Middle Child	• May feel crowded out, unsure of position. • May be sensitive, bitter or revengeful. • May be a good diplomat or mediator.	• Make time for one-on-one activities. • Include in family functions. • Ask for her opinion.
Youngest Child	• Often spoiled by parents and older siblings. • Often kept a baby. • Often self-indulgent. • Often highly creative. • Often clever.	• Do not do for the youngest (especially on a regular basis) what he can do alone. • Don't rescue from conflicts (thus making a victim). • Don't refer to as "the baby." • Encourage self-reliance.

As the chart shows, family constellation is another important building block. But this is important to understand: It is not so much the child's position in the family, but his view of the position that matters and makes a difference in the way he develops his personality. You and your children may or may not fit these typical characteristics, depending on decisions you have made.

The influence over which parents have the most control is their own style of parenting.

■ **Methods of parenting.** The influence over which parents have the most control is their own style of parenting. Let's review the three possible styles or methods:

1. **Autocratic Style (The Dictator):** The parent as dictator is an all-powerful figure who uses reward and punishment as tools for keeping everyone in line. Children are told what, how, where and when to do everything. There is very little room for them to question, challenge, or make their own decisions.

2. **Permissive Style (The Doormat):** The parent as doormat allows the children to "do their own thing" too often. There are few limits placed on children and little respect for order and routine. Many permissive parents behave as doormats, allowing their children to walk all over them. In such a system, children experience insecurity because there is no feeling of cooperation or belonging.

Active parenting is, in some respects, a balance between the autocratic and permissive methods, but it is much more.

3. **Democratic Style (The Active Parent):** Active parenting is, in some respects, a balance between the autocratic and permissive methods, but it is much more. In an active parenting household, parents and children have rights and responsibilities. The parent is the leader and encourages cooperation and stimulates learning. There is order and routine, and every person in the family is an important member of it.

Understanding Behavior: Purpose Not Cause

In order to understand another person's behavior, it does little good to look back and try to figure out what caused it. Humans are beings with free will. We choose how to behave based on our experience, values and goals for the future. So to understand why people, including children, behave the way they do, we always want to ask ourselves, "What is their goal?" "What is the 'payoff' their behavior is aimed at getting?"

For example, 10-year-old Janelle refused to clean up her mess in the family room after her father had told her to. Her father was angry and threatened to take away TV for a week. Janelle stormed out of the room saying, "It's not fair!"

Why has Janelle refused to comply with her father's order? What is her purpose or goal? Does her behavior get her the "payoff" she wants? To answer these questions, we want to look at four basic goals of all children's behavior, then see which one Janelle might achieve through her behavior.

Four Goals of Child Behavior

In Chapter One we said that the purpose of parenting was to protect and prepare our children to survive and to thrive in the kind of society in which they will live. Building on the foundation laid by Rudolf Dreikurs, *Active Parenting Today* suggests that there are four goals basic to human survival and the ability to thrive. These same four goals govern our children's behavior:

■ contact
■ power
■ protection
■ withdrawal

Let's look at each of these goals of human behavior more closely, particularly as they appear during the years of childhood.

Contact

The basic need of every human being is to belong.

The basic need of every human being is to belong. A baby could not survive without others to depend upon. Neither could the human species have survived throughout history without belonging to various groups: families, communities, cities, states and nations, to name a few.

Out of this desire to belong, each of us develops the goal of making contact—physical or emotional—with other human beings. For an infant, the need to be held is actually critical to its survival. Later, contact with Mom and Dad helps the growing child develop a sense of belonging in the family. The self-esteem and courage that grow out of this belonging make it possible for the child to make positive contact outside the family. Schools, religious organizations, sports leagues and other institutions offer additional opportunities for contact and belonging.

Power

Each one of us wants to influence our environment and gain at least a measure of control over it. We would like for things to go our way; we want the power to make that happen. It is through learning that we become able to do this. As the saying goes, "Knowledge is power." As parents, we want to empower our children to learn and to make positive contributions.

Protection

To survive and thrive we must be able to protect ourselves and our families. Our instinct to repel attacks—whether physical or psychological—has led to the development of elaborate systems of justice and defense. Yet it is by contributing to the well-being of others that our self-protection reaches its highest point. When we help our neighbor survive and thrive, our neighbor is less likely to become desperate and attack. Thus our own protection is enhanced.

Withdrawal

Time-outs are essential and refreshing in any sport. Just as a child seeks contact, at other times he needs to withdraw, regroup, center. Again, from our early survival instinct, we learned to withdraw from danger. Also, withdrawing is a kind of counterbalancing act to the goal of contact.

Positive and Negative Approaches to the Four Goals

There are no good or bad children, only those who choose to pursue four basic goals in either positive or negative ways.

Active Parenting Today has the belief that there are no good or bad children, only those who choose to pursue these four basic goals in either positive or negative ways. Children with high self-esteem and courage will generally choose the positive approaches. Those with low self-esteem who are discouraged will more likely choose the negative approaches. The following chart provides some labels we can use to distinguish these approaches:

Child's Goal	Positive Approach	Negative Approach
Contact	Contribution	Undue Attention-Seeking
Power	Independence	Rebellion
Protection	Assertiveness; forgiveness	Revenge
Withdrawal	Centering	Undue Avoidance

How To Determine a Child's Goal

Because parents do not usually know the goals behind a child's misbehavior, we often take an action that makes the problem worse. In other words, our discipline actually gives the child a payoff in terms of achieving her basic goal. And if negative behavior works, why not continue to use it? After all, it's usually the easier approach.

The first step, then, is to determine what your child really wants.

The first step, then, is to determine what your child really wants. Once we know the goal, we can help the child choose the positive approach to getting it. This requires some detective work on our part. There are two clues that will usually tell us the child's goal:

1. Our own feeling during a conflict: Are we annoyed, angry, hurt or helpless?

   Because much of our child's misbehavior is aimed at us, becoming aware of our own feelings during a conflict can be a powerful clue to his goals.

2. The child's response to our attempts at correcting the misbehavior.

   How does a child behave *after* we have made an effort to correct the misbehavior?

The chart on the following page is a guide for using this information:

If We Feel . . .	And the Child's Response to Correction Is to . . .	Then the Negative Approach Is . . .	To the Child's Goal of . . .
annoyed	stop, but start again very soon	undue attention-seeking	contact
angry	increase the misbehavior or give in only to fight again another day	rebellion	power
hurt	continue to hurt us or increase the misbehavior	revenge	protection
helpless	become passive; refuse to try	undue avoidance	withdrawal

Let's look more closely at each of the four negative approaches.

1. Undue Attention-Seeking

The child who seeks contact through undue attention-seeking probably has the mistaken belief that she must be the center of attention in order to belong. While young children will do things to get this attention from their parents, older children prefer the attention of peers. They may become class clowns or the ones who are constantly in trouble—anything to stay in the limelight.

So the child finds ways to keep people busy. The child may act forgetful, or helpless, or lazy, putting the parent in his service with reminders and coaxing. Or the child may get attention by clowning, asking constant questions, pestering or making a nuisance. Adults typically feel annoyed or irritated with such behavior. When we correct the child, he will usually stop the misbehavior. After all, our correction has given the contact the child seeks. However, the child will usually want more contact soon, and resume the misbehavior.

How parents pay off the negative approach of undue attention-seeking:
We tend to remind, nag, coax, complain, give mini-lectures, scold, and otherwise stay in contact with the child. This attention tends to reinforce the child's mistaken approach to achieving contact.

Act more and talk less.

What can parents do differently? The key to helping your child shift from the negative approach to the positive with any of the four goals is to do the unexpected. We have to break the pattern the child has come to expect, avoiding the "payoffs" that maintain the mistaken ideas. In the case of undue attention-seeking, we want to *act more and talk less*. The discipline that works best is either a brief confrontation through an "I" message or a logical consequence. (These techniques will be explained in Chapter Four.)

Discipline is only half the process for helping a child change approaches. It is designed to limit the negative behavior. However, just as important, we also want to actively encourage the child towards the positive approach. In the case of undue attention-seeking, we want to help the child achieve the recognition and contact she wants by playing a useful role. We can help find meaningful ways for the child to contribute to the group while ignoring some of the unproductive attention-getting behaviors. Using the encouragement skills learned in Chapter Two will help.

2. Rebellion

Of the four negative approaches, rebellion is the most common and creates the most distress in families and schools. The child who becomes discouraged trying to achieve his goal of power in a positive way can easily find power in the negative approach of rebellion. We talked earlier about how an autocratic parenting style tends to influence the child towards rebellion. This was the case in the example of Janelle and her father over the messy family room. His dictator style triggered Janelle's rebellious approach to power.

The child's mistaken belief with this approach is that the only way to achieve power is to control others, or at least show others she can't be controlled by them. This behavior can be very frustrating, and the typical feeling that clues us we are engaged in a power struggle is our own anger. If we express this anger to the child and join in the power struggle, the child's usual response is to intensify the struggle and even increase the misbehavior. If the child does back down during such a confrontation, it is only to fight again another day.

How parents pay off the negative approach of rebellion: There are two ways to lose a power struggle: 1) by fighting, and 2) by giving in. When we get angry and engage in a verbal fight, we are in effect saying to the child, "Look how powerful you are; you have made me angry and pulled me down to your level." When we give in to a rebelling child's unreasonable demands, we give the message, "Look how powerful your rebellion is; it has gotten you your way." Either way, the child's rebellious approach to power has been paid off, and will likely continue.

What can parents do differently? To successfully side-step the struggle for power, we must refuse to fight or give in. The parent who tends toward the dictator style can communicate more confidence in the child's ability to make decisions by himself. Rather than boss, we can give a choice. We can let the child make some mistakes, and then experience the consequences . . . without our lecturing or humiliating. We can set up family council meetings (Chapter Six) to involve the child in making decisions that affect the whole family. We can use the family enrichment activities, communication skills, and methods of encouragement described in this program to begin winning a more cooperative relationship. And, most important, we can show the child that we are not interested in fighting. Instead, we will work together to find solutions, and when discipline is necessary, we will use logical consequences (Chapter Four) rather than anger and punishment.

The parent who tends towards the doormat style, in addition to using the Active Parenting skills just described, can refuse to give in to the child's unreasonable demands. We can stop being short-order cooks, clean-up services, wake-up callers and last minute chauffeurs. We can set firm limits, negotiate within those limits, refuse to be intimidated by the displays of anger and enforce the consequences of breaking the limits (Chapter Four). We can let our children know that while we believe they should be treated respectfully, we expect to be treated respectfully as well.

3. Revenge

An increase in the power struggle usually leads to the negative approach of revenge, especially if the child feels that the parent has "won too many battles" or has hurt the child in the process. The child decides that the best form of protection is to hurt back. The parent's typical feeling is hurt, and because our autocratic tradition tells us that when children hurt us we should punish them more, an escalating revenge cycle begins.

Because as parents we want to see our children survive and thrive, we can never win this revenge war. All children have to do to hurt us is fail. They can fail at school; they can fail with peers; they can fail with drugs, with sex, and, ultimately, they can fail at life by committing suicide. The result each time is a parent left hurting.

How parents pay off the negative approach of revenge: When children seek to protect themselves by getting revenge, they are usually feeling very discouraged. When we retaliate with punishment and put-downs, we discourage them further and confirm their belief that they have a right to hurt us back. The more we hurt them, the more they want to hurt us back.

By refusing to hurt back, we can do the unexpected and break the cycle.

What can parents do differently? Someone has to stop the revenge cycle if the situation is to improve. We can stubbornly demand that the child change (which is what many of us have been taught to do), or we can play the leadership role in the family and call a cease-fire. By refusing to hurt back, we can do the unexpected and break the cycle.

It will help us to remember that no child is born "bad" or "mean." For children to act this way, they have to be hurting inside. The first step, then, is to do what we can to stop whatever is hurting the child. If it is our behavior, then we can take a new approach. If someone else is hurting her, we can support the child in handling it herself, or take more direct action when appropriate. Sometimes, however, the child has not been wronged but is hurting because of her misconception about how life ought to work. Perhaps we have coddled the child in the past, and now we have begun to treat the child (and ourselves) more respectfully. In these cases a calm and firm manner will help. Finally, the skills discussed for handling a power struggle will also be useful in redirecting a revenge-seeking child.

4. Undue Avoidance

Children who become extremely discouraged may sink so low in their own self-esteem that they give up trying. Their belief becomes "I can't succeed so I'll avoid trying; then I can't fail." They develop an apathy and lack of motivation that often leaves parents and educators feeling helpless. Such children may become truant from school, fail to do assignments, and avoid peers. In the teen years, tobacco, alcohol and other drugs may become a way for them to avoid the challenges life poses and to find temporary relief from their own discouragement.

How parents pay off the negative approach of undue avoidance: It is often our own perfectionism that causes the child's long slow slide into undue avoidance. When we focus excessively on mistakes, when nothing ever seems to be good enough for us, when all we talk about is his great "potential," the child may give up trying altogether.

Once a child has chosen avoidance, we often make the mistake of giving up on him. We write him off as a loser and stop making an effort to help. Or we yell and scream, humiliate and punish. Either way, we send the message "You're not good enough for us." This confirms the child's own evaluation of himself, and so justifies his avoidance.

Help the child find tasks that she can perform successfully.

What can parents do differently? Communicate to the child that whether she succeeds or fails, our love is unconditional. In addition to such acceptance of the child, we will need to practice patience and give a lot of encouragement. We can remind ourselves that the child is exaggerating her avoidance to see if the worst is true (that she really is as bad off as she thinks). We can help the child find tasks that she can perform successfully, so that she can begin to break the misconception of herself as a loser. And we can help her to see that mistakes are for learning, and failure is just a lesson on the road to success.

The chart on the following page summarizes our understanding of children's behavior:

Basic Goal of Child's Action	Child's Positive ⊕ or Negative ⊖ Approach to Goal	Child's Belief	Parent's Typical Feeling	Child's Response	Some Actions You Can Take
Contact	Recognition ⊕	My contributions are recognized. I belong by cooperating. I enjoy human contact.	Closeness	Cooperation and contribution.	Encourage cooperation, acknowledge the child's contributions.
Contact	Undue Attention-Seeking ⊖	I belong only when I'm noticed or served. The world must revolve around me.	Irritation	Stops, but begins again very soon.	Ignore the behavior. Give the child full attention at other times. Use logical and natural consequences; act, don't talk.
Power	Independence ⊕	I am able to influence what happens to me. I am responsible for my life.	Admiration	Responsible, self-motivated behavior, learning.	Give responsibilities. Continue to encourage.
Power	Rebellion ⊖	I belong only when I'm the boss or when I'm showing you that you can't boss me.	Anger	Escalates behavior or gives in only to fight again another day.	Remove yourself from the conflict. Talk about it after cooling off period. Don't fight or give in. Take sail out of child's wind.
Protection	Assertiveness, forgiveness ⊕	When attacked or treated unfairly, I can stand up for myself and those I love. I am able to forgive and even contribute to those who have wronged me.	Love	Positive contact.	Express your own positive feelings; demonstrate assertiveness and forgiveness in your own relationships.
Protection	Revenge ⊖	I've been hurt and will get even by hurting back. Then maybe they'll learn they can't get away with hurting me!	Hurt	To continue to hurt, or escalate misbehavior.	Refuse to be hurt. Withdraw from the conflict. Show love to vengeful child. Avoid temptation to hurt back.
Withdrawal	Centering ⊕	There are times when I need to be alone. And there are situations to be left alone.	Respect	Resumes contact when ready.	Respect the child's wishes to be alone. Don't press. Later, use active communication.
Withdrawal	Avoidance ⊖	I'm a failure at everything. Leave me alone. Expect nothing from me.	Helplessness	Becomes passive; refuses to try; gives up.	Be patient; find ways to encourage child.

The Parent-Child Cycle

When we presented the think-feel-do cycle in Chapter Two, we explained that many people act as if other people controlled their feelings. For example:

"You make me angry."
"You make me so happy."

Although other people do *influence* or trigger our feelings, the *cause* of our feelings is our own beliefs, attitudes and values—what we think:

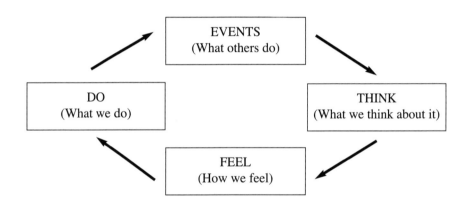

We influence others through our behavior and they influence us through theirs. The choice, however, is always with us. One benefit of accepting responsibility for our own thoughts, feelings and behavior is that we become more independent and personally powerful.

Example: "You're really making me angry" says to a child whose mistaken approach to power is rebellion, "Look how powerful your rebellion is: it has made me lose my temper." This actually reinforces the child's mistaken belief, and he rebels even more.

Example: Accepting that "I have a choice: I can either get angry or I can take some other action" puts you in control of yourself. When you "push your own buttons" instead of giving away that power, many alternatives become available.

By combining two think-feel-do cycles, we can see how parents and children influence each other, while still making their own choices. Remember, since it is a cycle, it does not matter where you begin. Each step will influence all the others.

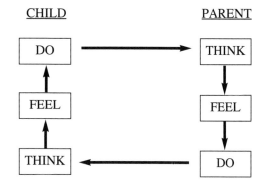

We can see how what a child might "*do*" can influence what his parent thinks. The parent's thinking then influences his feeling, which influences what he chooses to do. What the parent does then influences what the child thinks, feels and does . . . which influences what the parent thinks . . . and around and around it goes until the two physically separate (which is what is meant by "taking your sail out of the child's wind"—often a good course of action in a power struggle).

We can also see how our understanding of the child's behavior and our style of parenting fit into this cycle:

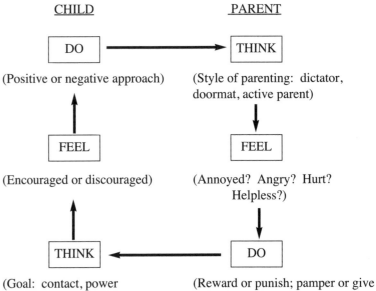

CHILD   PARENT

DO   ⟶   THINK

(Positive or negative approach)   (Style of parenting: dictator, doormat, active parent)

FEEL   FEEL

(Encouraged or discouraged)   (Annoyed? Angry? Hurt? Helpless?)

THINK   ⟵   DO

(Goal: contact, power protection, withdrawal)   (Reward or punish; pamper or give in; use Active Parenting skills.)

Example: Janelle refuses to clean up the family room when her father asks her to. Let's see what this looks like in the parent-child cycle:

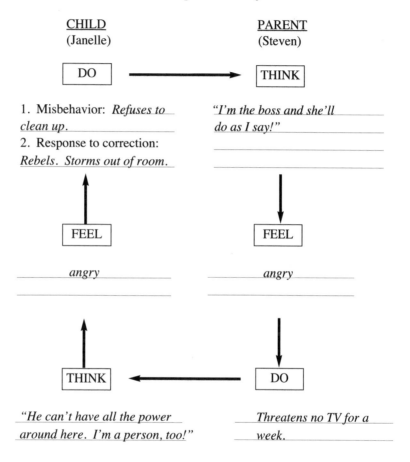

CHILD
(Janelle)

PARENT
(Steven)

DO → THINK

1. Misbehavior: *Refuses to clean up.*
2. Response to correction: *Rebels. Storms out of room.*

"I'm the boss and she'll do as I say!"

FEEL

FEEL

angry

angry

THINK ← DO

"He can't have all the power around here. I'm a person, too!"

Threatens no TV for a week.

Remember, we want to change negative cycles to positive ones by encouraging our children to choose positive approaches to their goals—instead of misbehavior. In the previous example, Steve's anger and punishment only serve to reinforce Janelle's negative approach to power. Her rebellion drew him into a power struggle. ("Look how powerful I am; I got him angry!") Since the key to breaking these old cycles that have become so familiar to our children is to do the unexpected, we need to learn how to avoid getting angry so easily. Then, we can utilize the discipline skills presented in Chapter Four to effectively correct their misbehavior.

Parenting and Anger

Anger (and its expression) has long been a subject of conflict between parents and children. Anger seems to be natural, and yet it is often so destructive that we are not quite sure what to make of it. Perhaps these pages will give you a new view of an old subject.

What Does Anger Mean?

- **Response to frustration.** Anger is an emotional and physiological response to frustration. If an important need, want or desire is blocked for us, our bodies and emotions react with intense feelings that we often label as anger.

  For example, a caveman, walking through the woods, comes upon a fallen tree that blocks his path. On the other side of the tree are some berries he wants to pick and eat. He strains to push the fallen tree aside, but he isn't strong enough, and he becomes frustrated at the thought of not reaching his goal. His frustration produces physiological responses that enable him to lift the fallen tree savagely and hurl it aside.

- **Purpose of anger.** Anger releases certain chemicals into our bloodstream. These chemicals produce changes that make us stronger, faster, and look intimidating. This added power may help us remove whatever block is frustrating us.

- **Old brain-new brain.** Anger is associated with the so-called "old brain," which has been present in human beings for millions of years. But as the "new brain" has evolved around the old brain, so has human intelligence. This gives us the ability to handle problems with solutions other than brute force.

■ **"Use," not "lose" our temper.** Rudolf Dreikurs once said that people do not "lose" their temper; they "use" their temper. What he meant was that people sometimes use anger to intimidate others into giving them what they want. Since this often damages the relationship and is hurtful, we want to find positive ways to "use" our temper.

How To Use Anger Positively

■ **The message of anger.** Our own angry feelings tell us that one of our goals is being blocked. It also sends clearly this message:

"Act! Don't just sit there; get up and do something."

If we do something soon, we can often solve the problem before it gets worse, and before we blow up. If we don't act but try to ignore the message, several things could happen:

1. The problem might go away by other means, but this is a risky and uncertain possibility.

2. Our anger may grow in intensity until it propels us into some action, which is likely to be desperate and unthinking.

3. Our anger will seethe internally, expressing itself in unexpected ways: headaches, rashes, ulcers, even heart attacks.

■ **How to act on anger.** We can act in one of three ways when dealing with anger:

1. **Act to change the situation.** (*Do* something different.)

   Example: Struggle until you remove the fallen tree.

   Example: Use effective discipline skills such as the "I" messages and logical consequences that appear in Chapter Four.

2. **Reduce the importance of the goal.** Put it in perspective. (*Think* something different.)

   Example: Although you may want the berries very much, be aware that you don't need them for your survival.

Example: Your child refuses to take a bath. Remind yourself that your goal of a daily bath is less important than your good relationship with your child.

3. **Change your goals.** Find an alternative. (Again, think something different.)

Example: Decide you don't really care that much about the berries or find an alternative that will satisfy your need . . . an apple tree near the river.

Example: Give up *your* goal of having your child play the piano and encourage an alternative activity of her choice.

Helping Children Use Their Anger

Because children are usually more primitive in their expression of emotions, they will often resemble the caveman when experiencing frustration and anger. Tantrums and hitting are fairly common with young children. There are several ways parents can help:

1. **Give them a good model.** The way you handle your own problems and frustrations will provide a model for your children.

   ■ Do you fly into a rage, hurling insults and humiliating remarks?
   ■ Do you strike out at others?
   ■ Do you sink into a depression (an adult temper tantrum or "silent storm")?

2. **Guide them with words to find more effective forms of expression.**

   Example: "You have the right to feel the way you do, but in our family, we don't scream and blame; we look for solutions."

   Example: "I can see that you are angry. Can you tell me with words instead of hitting?"

   Example: "When you get angry at me, please tell me without calling me names. I don't call you names; please don't call me names."

3. **Remove yourself from a power struggle.** When children have tantrums, you can acknowledge their anger, but at the same time "take your sails out of their wind." Don't try to overpower the child; withdraw instead. This action says to the child, "I am not intimidated by your show of temper and will not give in, but I won't punish or humiliate you either." The result is that children who get neither a fight nor their own way after throwing tantrums will usually find more acceptable ways to influence people.

4. **Give your child a choice.** In those situations where a child's tantrum interferes with the rights of others (e.g., in a restaurant, or when company is in the home), the child can be given the choice of either expressing himself appropriately or having a tantrum someplace else. You must be ready to act on the child's choice by calmly and firmly removing the child if the tantrum persists.

5. **Allow your child to influence your decisions.** When a person feels powerless to influence leaders, frustration gives way to anger and rebellion. If you allow your child to influence your decisions concerning her, she will also not be as likely to resort to such unconscious tactics as bedwetting, soiling and stomach disorders, to name a few.

The method your child uses to influence your decisions will be influenced by what you allow to work. If you "give in" to tantrums, whining or tears, the child will learn to use these tactics again. If you redirect your child to express his anger respectfully, listen to his arguments, and sometimes change your decisions, then your child learns the important skill of negotiation.

Family Enrichment Activity

Teaching Skills

Part of developing self-esteem and courage is seeing oneself as a capable individual. When you take the time to teach your child a skill, you not only help her become more capable, but also give her positive ways of achieving the goal of power. In fact, teaching your child a skill empowers her in a very positive way and enriches your relationship with her.

The following steps can help you teach a skill effectively:

1. **Motivate:** Encourage your child to *want* to learn the skill by explaining the value the skill has to the child or the entire family. For example:

   "Once you learn how to make your own sandwich for lunch, you won't always have to wait for me. Maybe sometimes you could even help me make lunch for everyone."

2. **Select a good time:** Pick a time when neither you nor your child will be rushed or upset by other things.

3. **Break the skill down into small (A to Z) steps:** When skills are learned one step at a time, there are more successes to help build courage and motivation. For example:

   "The first step is to get all of the ingredients out on the counter: the bread, the peanut butter, the honey and a knife."

4. **Demonstrate:** Show your child how to perform the skill, explaining slowly as you do. For example:

   "Next, watch how I dip the knife into the peanut butter, then slowly spread it onto a piece of bread."

5. **Let your child try:** Let your child perform the skill while you stand by, ready to offer help if he needs it. Be gentle about mistakes, and let it be fun. For example:

   "Okay, now you try it. Just dip the knife in the jar so that you get plenty of that yummy peanut butter on it."

6. **Encourage, encourage, encourage:** Make plenty of encouraging comments that acknowledge your child's efforts and results. For example:

   "Great! That's the way to do it."

7. **Work or play together:** Once your child has learned the skill, you can sometimes work or play together, so that you can both enjoy the companionship of the activity. For example:

   "Let's eat!"

Family Enrichment Activity
Teaching Skills

List the names of your children and what skill you have decided to teach each child:

Child's Name   Skill To Be Taught

1. _____   _____

2. _____   _____

3. _____   _____

After you teach the skill, use the seven steps as a checklist:

	Child	1	2	3
1. Did you motivate the child?		❑	❑	❑
2. Did you select a good time when you weren't rushed?		❑	❑	❑
3. Did you break the skill down into A to Z steps?		❑	❑	❑
4. Did you demonstrate how to do this job?		❑	❑	❑
5. Did you let him or her try?		❑	❑	❑
6. Did you encourage?		❑	❑	❑
7. Did you work alongside your child?		❑	❑	❑

What went well with each child?

1. _____

2. _____

3. _____

What might you do to improve the experience next time? _____

_____

The Parent-Child Cycle

Video #2: Janelle - Negative

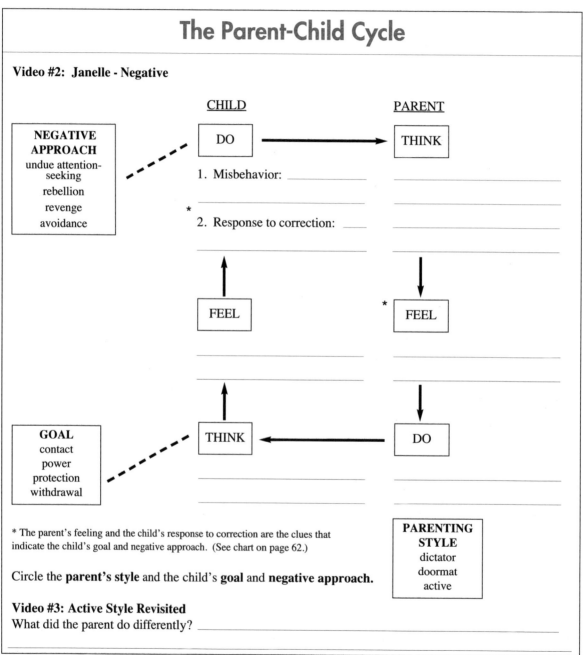

CHILD   PARENT

NEGATIVE APPROACH
undue attention-seeking
rebellion
revenge
avoidance

DO   →   THINK

1. Misbehavior: _____

* 2. Response to correction: ___

FEEL   * FEEL

GOAL
contact
power
protection
withdrawal

THINK   ←   DO

* The parent's feeling and the child's response to correction are the clues that
indicate the child's goal and negative approach. (See chart on page 62.)

Circle the **parent's style** and the child's **goal** and **negative approach.**

PARENTING STYLE
dictator
doormat
active

Video #3: Active Style Revisited
What did the parent do differently? _____

Four Goals Video Practice

Video #4: Zack - Negative

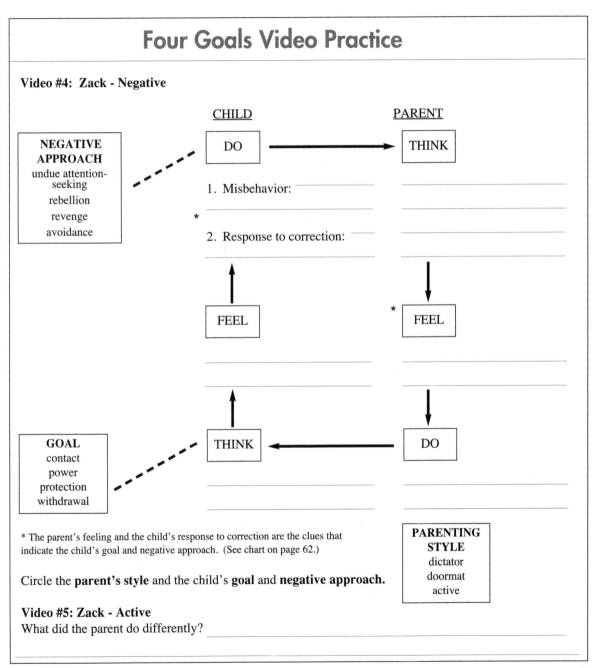

CHILD   PARENT

NEGATIVE APPROACH
undue attention-seeking
rebellion
revenge
avoidance

DO   →   THINK

1. Misbehavior:

* 2. Response to correction:

FEEL   * FEEL

GOAL
contact
power
protection
withdrawal

THINK   ←   DO

* The parent's feeling and the child's response to correction are the clues that indicate the child's goal and negative approach. (See chart on page 62.)

Circle the **parent's style** and the child's **goal** and **negative approach**.

PARENTING STYLE
dictator
doormat
active

Video #5: Zack - Active
What did the parent do differently?

Four Goals Video Practice

Video #6: Jade - Negative

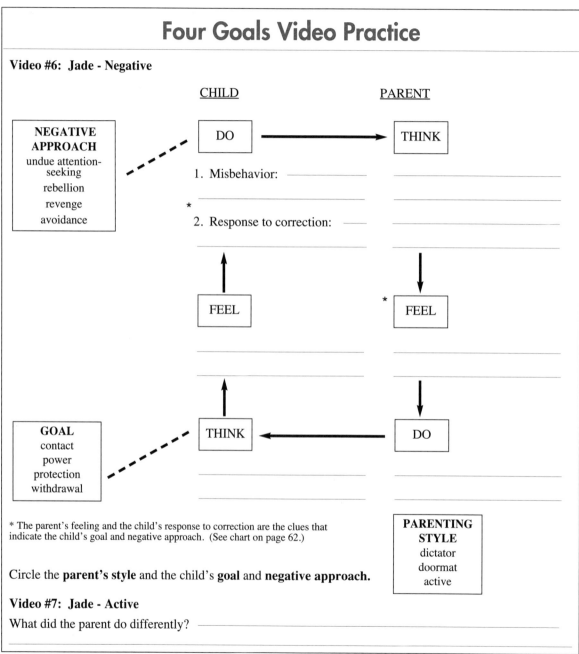

CHILD   PARENT

NEGATIVE APPROACH
undue attention-seeking
rebellion
revenge
avoidance

DO → THINK

1. Misbehavior: _____

* _____

2. Response to correction: _____

FEEL   * FEEL

GOAL
contact
power
protection
withdrawal

THINK ← DO

* The parent's feeling and the child's response to correction are the clues that indicate the child's goal and negative approach. (See chart on page 62.)

PARENTING STYLE
dictator
doormat
active

Circle the **parent's style** and the child's **goal** and **negative approach.**

Video #7: Jade - Active

What did the parent do differently? _____

80

Four Goals Video Practice

Video #8: Ramon - Negative

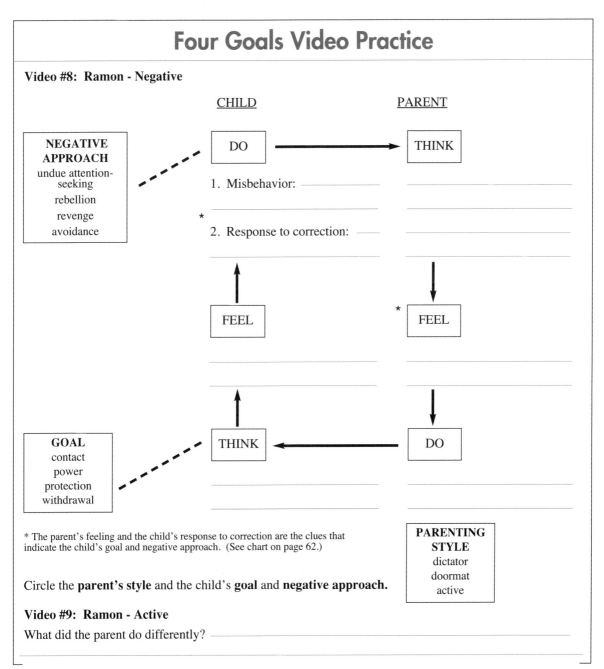

CHILD   PARENT

NEGATIVE APPROACH
undue attention-seeking
rebellion
revenge
avoidance

DO → THINK

1. Misbehavior: _____

*

2. Response to correction: _____

FEEL   * FEEL

GOAL
contact
power
protection
withdrawal

THINK ← DO

* The parent's feeling and the child's response to correction are the clues that indicate the child's goal and negative approach. (See chart on page 62.)

Circle the **parent's style** and the child's **goal** and **negative approach.**

PARENTING STYLE
dictator
doormat
active

Video #9: Ramon - Active

What did the parent do differently? _____

Four Goals Home Observation
Analyzing the Problem Activity

Observe the next conflict you have with your child from the point of view of the parent-child cycle and the four goals of behavior. Then answer these questions:

What was my child's misbehavior? _____

_____

What did I do to try to correct it? _____

_____

How did my child respond to what I did to correct it? _____

_____

How did I feel during the conflict? _____

_____

What was my child's goal? (See chart on page 62.) _____

_____

What was my child's negative approach to this goal? _____

_____

Did I pay off this negative approach? If so, how? _____

_____

If not, what did I do differently to redirect him to the positive approach? _____

_____

Chapter Three. Home Activities Checklist

(Check when completed.)

❏ 1. Read Chapter Three. If you wish to read ahead, please do so.

❏ 2. Teach a skill to each child (or begin teaching) and complete the Family Enrichment Activity guide sheet on page 77.

❏ 3. Complete the Four Goals Home Observation guide sheet on page 82.

❏ 4. Call your buddy (optional).

Notes _____

_____

_____

_____

_____

_____

_____

_____

_____

_____

_____

_____

_____

_____

_____

_____

Developing
Responsibility

There was a young man who was desperate for work. He had never had a job, and though he was 27 years old, his parents were still supporting him. They had finally had enough of his dependency, as well as their own overprotection, and had given him three months to find a job. When he saw after 10 weeks that they were not bluffing about pushing him out of the nest, he began seriously beating the pavement for work.

He failed. He had never been taught to do things for himself and had not developed the skills to find a job. His father, as usual, came to his rescue. He called a friend in the construction business who arranged for the son to have a job driving a dump truck, a job for which he would be well paid. On the first day of his first job, the young man backed the dump truck over an embankment. When confronted by the foreman and asked how he could do such a reckless thing, the young man replied, "Well, nobody told me not to."

This chapter and the next will present methods of handling problems and misbehavior when they occur in a family. But this chapter is also about something much more basic to the development of a child's ability to thrive in our democratic society. It is about responsibility.

Responsibility

The more responsible we become, the more effective and satisfied with our circumstances we also become.

How much responsibility for the course of our lives do we accept? If the answer is "less than total responsibility," then we are cheating ourselves. The more responsible we become, the more effective and satisfied with our circumstances we also become.

Why do we avoid responsibility if this is so? Because we are afraid of being blamed or punished for making mistakes. Who would blame or punish us? Sometimes it is critical people with whom we live or work. But even their criticism would be harmless if it were not for the fact that we blame and punish ourselves the hardest.

Where did we learn this self-criticism? Most of us learned it a long time ago from our parents, many of whom believed in the autocratic or permissive methods of parenting and the blame and criticism that went with these styles.

How do we avoid responsibility? We blame others for our mistakes and failures, or we blame circumstances, because it is too painful to accept responsibility ourselves and suffer the self-criticism we insist on dishing out.

We say, "You made me late," or "You made me angry." Or we justify our failings: "Being late isn't such a big deal"; "I have a bad temper"; "I'm a Leo"; "I'm an alcoholic"; "I'm just no good"; "Nobody told me not to."

How can we help prepare children for responsible adulthood? The first step is for us to resist the temptation to blame and punish them for their mistakes and misbehavior. These techniques actually influence them to avoid responsibility—to blame and justify. This chapter is about other methods of disciplining children, methods that teach responsibility while they help you handle everyday problems. But first, let's look at what responsibility really is:

Responsibility is the process of making choices and accepting the consequences of those choices.

The most effective and the most satisfied people have learned how to make choices and accept responsibility for whatever happens as a result of their choices. If the consequence is positive, then they have a good model for making a similar choice in the future. If the consequence is not satisfying, then they know better how to choose next time and avoid the same consequences. Either way, they learn and grow. And this is the way children learn and grow, too.

An essential condition for responsibility is the freedom to choose.

In this chapter, we will look at some effective, tried-and-true methods that parents have used to help their children improve in their ability to make responsible choices. But first, let's look at the circumstances in which choices are made.

Freedom and the Limits to Freedom

A choice can be made only when there is freedom to choose. For if the person is not free to choose, we have to assume that someone else has already made the choice for the person. An essential condition for responsibility, therefore, is the freedom to choose.

Dictator parents give their children almost no freedom to make choices. They believe that since children lack experience, parents must make the choices for them. They may want to help their children avoid the pain and pitfalls of poor choices. However, parents who follow a dictator model of parenting stifle their child's ability to handle responsibility. The child eventually rebels against these strict limits, and yet remains inexperienced at making choices on his own. The results are both the pain and pitfalls the parent sought to avoid.

Doormat parents follow a model of parenting that resembles lawlessness. Such parents allow their children too much freedom to choose. Yet without structure and limits, children do not learn responsibility any better in these circumstances than in an autocratic home.

A young man executed in the electric chair for the murder of a woman and her three small children reported that he would probably do it again if he had the chance, because he came from a home where no one ever told him not to do certain things. He had grown up without limits—free to do whatever he pleased. And was he happy about this? Hardly. He chose the electric chair instead of imprisonment because he described his life as a "living hell"!

So children clamor for freedom to make their own choices, while parents call for limits to that freedom, and the dialogue becomes a universal chant, repeated the world over:

> "Freedom!"
> "Limits."
> "FREEDOM!"
> "LIMITS!"

Active parents are acutely aware of their children's need for freedom, but within well-defined limits.

Fortunately, there is a third alternative—"active" parenting. Active parents are acutely aware of their children's need for freedom, but within well-defined limits. They work hard to set limits in line with each child's age and level of responsibility, aware that over-restrictive limits lead to sneaking around and other forms of rebellion, and limits too loose lead to selfish and destructive behavior.

This concept of "freedom within expanding limits" suggests that a 2-year-old will make fewer of her own decisions than a 9-year-old, who again will make fewer decisions than a 17-year-old. In fact, the ideal situation for a child spending her last year at home is for the teen to make almost all of her own decisions. The parent has become almost like a roommate and consultant. This makes sense when we consider that our goal is to prepare children for independent living, because we won't always be around to provide limits.

Like most things, teaching responsibility is a gradual process. It involves giving children choices and then allowing them to experience the consequences of those choices. In fact, since responsibility is a matter of accepting the consequences of our choices, then a reasonable formula for teaching responsibility to children is:

R = C + C

Responsibility = Choice + Consequence

Misbehavior is a problem, but it is also an opportunity for teaching responsibility and problem solving.

What are our best opportunities for using this formula? First, we can let the child make more daily decisions. We can allow increasing freedom to make choices about what to eat and what to wear, for example, keeping in mind the child's age and stage of development. (Refer to "The Method of Choice" section in Chapter One.) Second, when we have a problem with the child's behavior, we can look for opportunities to give her choices. Misbehavior is a problem, but as we'll see in the next section, it is also an opportunity for teaching responsibility and problem solving.

The Problem-Handling Model for Parents

The difference between successful families and those constantly in pain and turmoil is not the presence or absence of problems. All families have problems and conflicts, and all children present challenges. The difference is in the ability of the family to successfully handle their problems so that learning occurs. The following diagram depicts a successful method of dealing with family problems.

The Problem-Handling Model

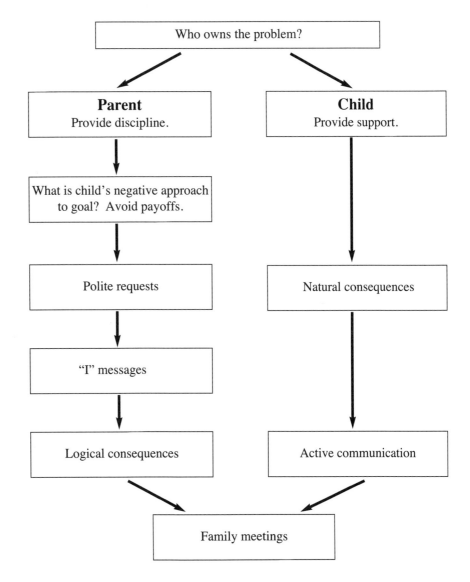

Who owns the problem?

Parent
Provide discipline.

Child
Provide support.

What is child's negative approach to goal? Avoid payoffs.

Polite requests

Natural consequences

"I" messages

Logical consequences

Active communication

Family meetings

ENCOURAGE . . . ENCOURAGE . . . ENCOURAGE.

You may have noticed that these same skills we use to handle everyday family problems are also the skills that enable us to teach our children courage, responsibility, cooperation and self-esteem. In this chapter we will cover problem prevention, problem ownership, natural and logical consequences, and "I" messages. Then in Chapter Five, we'll deal with active communication, and in Chapter Six, types of family meetings.

Who Owns the Problem?

This may seem a strange question to ask, but it is an important one. Dictators tend to act as if they own all of the problems in the family and are responsible for deciding what will be done to solve them. Doormats tend to take on too little responsibility for problems and allow their children too much freedom.

The active parent, however, understands there are some problems that belong to the child, and that the child should be free to decide how he will handle them. In those cases the parent may offer support and encouragement, but will not take over the problem. The active parent also understands the need for discipline when the problem belongs to the parent.

We can usually determine who owns a problem by asking three questions:

■ With whom is this behavior or situation interfering directly?

■ Who is raising the issue or making the complaint?

■ Whose goals are being blocked by the problem?

Let's look at some examples on the following page to help clarify this concept.

Situation	Who Owns Problem?	Why?
Children are giggling and noisy at a restaurant.	Parent	Parents are eating in a public place and the children's noise is disturbing other patrons and interfering with parents' enjoyment of their meal.
Your child rides her bike on a busy street.	Parent	It is the parents' responsibility to teach their children to use things safely; this situation isn't safe.
Your daughter doesn't like her sister going into her room without asking.	Child	Siblings are entitled to have a relationship with each other without parents interfering. They need to learn to work out together how they can best get along.
Your child complains that the teacher picks on him.	Child	Children have relationships with other adults. They need to learn how to relate to them on their own.
Your child has a temper tantrum in the supermarket.	Parent	The child's behavior is interfering with the parent's goal of shopping.
Your child doesn't complete his chore of setting the table.	Parent	The parent's goal of serving dinner is blocked.

Preventing Problems

Many conflicts and misunderstandings can be prevented if we will take the time to discuss guidelines and expectations before the situation occurs.

Children often misbehave simply because they don't know what we expect from them in the situation. In other words, they don't know where the limits are and how much freedom they are allowed. Of course, many a shrewd child will intentionally stay in the dark about the rules, operating on the belief that "it is easier to gain forgiveness than permission." In either case, many conflicts and misunderstandings can be prevented if we will take the time to discuss guidelines and expectations before the situation occurs.

Example: You have decided to take your 5-year-old grocery shopping with you. Talking with her before you leave home can improve your chances for having a problem-free outing and may save you a lot of time—and stress—in the store. Here are some tips for such a prevention discussion:

1. **Avoid laying down the law.** A dictator might present the rules to the child as though they were written in stone, but an active parent will be somewhat flexible. While we do have our limits, we can also listen to the child's wants, and allow for some choice within those limits.

   For example, you want your child to sit in the cart so you can keep an eye on her. She argues that she is now too big to sit in the cart. You agree she can walk along with you as long as she stays close by. If she wanders off, she must sit in the cart as agreed.

2. **Anticipate problems.** If you have been in similar situations before, then you probably know where the trouble spots will be. Otherwise, use your experience of similar situations and your knowledge of your child to anticipate the problems. Then discuss your expectations for these areas, getting agreement from your child about the rules.

   For example, your child often whines for a toy whenever you are in a store. Get agreement beforehand about how much money, if any, she will have to spend.

3. **Make the situation a win-win for both of you.** When discussing guidelines with your child, keep in mind that it is easier to comply with the rules if you enjoy the situation. We aren't suggesting the use of rewards or bribes for cooperative behavior, but rather to include some incentives.

   For example, avoid "If you'll be good, I'll buy you a toy." This is a bribe or a reward, and will lead to having to buy the child something every time you go to the store.

   Better: "If we finish our shopping by 4:30, we'll have time to do that puzzle together when we get home."

   Best: "How would you like to help me do the shopping by handing me the groceries off the shelf? Maybe you can help me decide some things you'd like to have for dinner."

Effective Discipline

Of course, we won't be able to prevent all problems. Children at times will become discouraged and turn to the negative approaches to their goals. When undue attention-seeking, rebellion, revenge or avoidance becomes their approach, their behavior will sometimes require discipline. An important point about discipline: *Discipline can either make a problem better or worse.*

Discipline that pays off a child's misbehavior by allowing the child to take a negative approach to his basic goal (contact, power, protection or withdrawal) will influence the child to continue the misbehavior or even increase it. Discipline that does not provide such a payoff can help redirect the child towards using positive approaches to attaining his goals.

Our goal is to teach our children, not to hurt them.

You may recall in Chapter One that we presented the case against using punishment as a means of influencing children in our modern society. We suggested that punishment (the idea that you have to hurt the child to teach him) often leads to resentment and revenge. Although problems may seem to get better in the short run, they usually become worse later on. In addition, punishment teaches nothing about responsibility, only about doing what you are told, or more often, finding sneaky ways not to get caught. There are four key things to keep in mind about discipline:

1. Our goal is to teach our children, not to hurt them. In fact, the word "discipline" itself comes from the Latin word "disciplina," meaning "instruction." Of course, our children may not like our instructions or the consequences we apply. However, they will not suffer hurt to either their bodies or their self-esteem in the process.

2. Whenever we discipline a child for negative behavior, we want to find opportunities to *encourage* any improvement the child makes.

3. When using discipline to influence our children, we always want to use the least assertive method that will work.

4. Come from caring when you discipline. When a child knows that you are disciplining her because you care about her, it's easier to accept. When we discipline out of frustration, anger and our own desires, it's difficult for the child to accept or "learn" the lesson we're trying to teach.

Polite Requests

Not every problem or conflict requires a full-fledged discussion or firm discipline. Often, a polite request is enough to influence a child to change behavior (especially if the relationship is already a positive one).

When a child doesn't know what we want in a situation, the first step is to politely make our desires known through a request. For example, you have decided that you no longer want to pamper your child by picking up the dirty dishes he leaves in the den. Your polite request might be, "Honey, from now on will you do me a favor and bring your dishes to the sink when you're through with your snack?" If your child agrees, be sure to add, "Thanks, that will be a big help." This may seem too obvious to mention, but we parents do talk to children in ways that would be clearly disrespectful if used with other adults. The parent in the above example could easily wait until she is fed up with being a servant, hold it inside for another week to let it really boil, then burst out with "I'm sick and tired of having to pick up your mess! What do you think I am, your personal servant? If you weren't so lazy and inconsiderate . . ." This kind of outburst is not likely to produce responsibility, cooperation or dishes in the sink.

If a child does comply with our polite request, but slips up, we can offer a friendly reminder: "Honey, I notice you forgot to put your dishes in the sink. Please come get them."

When a child repeatedly forgets to keep an agreement, when she isn't putting out the effort or is taking a negative approach to one of the four goals, then a stronger communication is called for.

"I" Messages

"I" messages, a term coined by psychologist Thomas Gordon in his pioneering Parent Effectiveness Training (P.E.T.) program, are firm and friendly communications that can produce surprisingly effective results. They are called "I" messages because they shift the emphasis from the child (a traditional "you" message) to how the parent ("I") feels about the child's behavior.

Here are some benefits of "I" messages:

- They allow the parent to say how he or she feels about the child's behavior without blaming or labeling the child.

- They create a situation in which the child is more likely to hear what the parent is saying because it is expressed in a nonthreatening way.

- They convey clearly to the child one consequence (the parent's feeling) of the child's behavior.

- They put the emphasis on the child's behavior and not on the child's personality.

- They give the child clear information about what change in behavior the parent wants.

When To Use an "I" Message:

"I" messages are only effective when the parent owns the problem. When a polite request has failed to change behavior, an "I" message is a more assertive next step. If the problem remains after an "I" message, then the use of logical consequences provides a third level of assertiveness.

Since "I" messages work best in a firm and calm tone of voice, avoid using them when you are too angry. Allow for a cooling-off period, then approach your child when you have regained control. An angry "I" message can easily trigger rebellion in a power-seeking child.

How To Send an "I" Message:

There are four parts to an "I" message.

1. Name the behavior or situation you want changed.
As we said in Chapter Two on encouragement, it is important to separate the deed from the doer. It isn't that the child is bad, only that we have a problem with something the child is doing. By beginning with a statement aimed at the behavior, we avoid attacking the child's personality and self-esteem. We begin this part with "When you . . ." or "I have a problem with . . ." For example:

"I have a problem with your leaving dirty dishes on the coffee table."

2. Say how you feel about the situation.

This lets the child know that the problem is serious to you (without your raising your voice). Although parents often use the word "angry" to describe their feelings, this is often a mask for two other emotions: "fear" and "hurt." Children can usually hear us better when we are expressing these emotions because they are less threatening. "I feel concerned" or "I feel hurt" may be closer to the truth, as well as more effective. This part of the "I" message begins with "I feel . . ." For example:

"I feel taken advantage of . . . "

3. State your reason.

Nobody likes to be treated as if he were expected to be blindly obedient. If we are going to change what is comfortable to us to please an authority, we at least want that authority to have a good reason. Children are no exception. A simple explanation about how the child's behavior is interfering with your purposes or the needs of the situation is called for. You can say, "because . . ." For example:

". . . because I have to spend time and energy cleaning up behind you."

4. Say what you want done.

You have already made a polite request or two, so now you are getting more assertive. This means letting your child know exactly what you would like done. Remember, you get more of what you ask for than what you don't ask for. This step can begin with "I want" or "I would like." For example:

"I would like you to bring your dirty dishes to the kitchen and put them in the dishwasher when you leave the den."

Putting this "I" message all together, we have this:

"I have a problem with your leaving dirty dishes on the coffee table. I feel taken advantage of because I have to spend time and energy cleaning up behind you. I would like you to bring your dirty dishes to the kitchen and put them in the dishwasher when you leave the den."

"I" Messages: Two Variations

1. Getting agreement: "Will you please . . ."

We can make an "I" message even stronger by getting an agreement from the child about the behavior we want changed. This can be done following the "I" message by simply adding the question, "Will you do that?" and then not moving until you get a "yes." This can also be done by changing the last step of the "I" message from "I would like . . ." to "Will you please . . ." For example:

"I have a problem with your leaving dirty dishes on the coffee table. I feel taken advantage of because I have to spend time and energy cleaning up behind you. Will you please bring your dirty dishes to the kitchen and put them in the dishwasher when you are finished?"

2. Establishing a time frame: "When?"

Every parent knows the frustrations of getting an agreement from a child about doing something, finding it still not done hours later, and confronting the child only to hear the refrain, "I'll do it." The implication, of course, is "I'll do it when I get around to it," and that may not occur in this century.

The solution is to get a clear agreement as to when the behavior will be completed. In the above example, the "when" is built into the phrase "when you are finished." Other times, it can be added right after the child agrees to the request by simply asking, "When?"

Natural and Logical Consequences

In order to influence a child to change from a negative behavior to a positive one, the child first needs clear information from the parent about what change is expected. "I" messages are a good clear way to do this. However, children sometimes need to experience a more concrete consequence of their actions in order to learn the lesson.

What is the value of consequences?

Children learn responsibility when they are given three things:

- ■ **Participation:** The opportunity to participate in setting the guidelines for their behavior.

- **Choice:** The opportunity to choose how to behave.

- **Consequences:** The opportunity to experience the logical results of their choice of behavior.

Consequences are powerful teachers about the effectiveness of our choices and behavior. Better than a punishment or lecture, consequences offer parents their prime discipline tools. There are two types of consequences: natural consequences and logical consequences.

Natural Consequences

Natural consequences are the results that naturally occur from a child's behavior without the parent doing anything.

Here are some examples:

- The natural consequence of not eating breakfast is getting hungry before lunch.

- The natural consequence of oversleeping on a school day is being late for school.

- The natural consequence of leaving your bicycle outside may be that it gets rusty or that it is stolen.

Natural consequences are particularly effective teachers because the parent can be a sympathetic third party, rather than the disciplinarian. Of course, to be effective we have to avoid two temptations: 1) to rescue (for example, buy him a new bike); and 2) to say "I told you so." (How much better to say, "Gee, I know that's frustrating," rather than "I told you this would happen if you didn't put that bike away!")

When Natural Consequences Cannot Be Used as Teachers

There are many situations when our best course of action is to stay out of the way and let the natural consequences teach the lesson. However, there are three circumstances in which a responsible parent cannot simply allow Mother Nature to take her toll:

1. When the natural consequences may be catastrophic. For example, the natural consequences of running into a busy street may be death.

2. When the natural consequences are so far into the future that the child is not concerned about the connection. For example, the natural consequences of not brushing her teeth may lead to eventual tooth decay.

3. When the natural consequences of a child's behavior affect others rather than the child. For example, the child borrows your scissors and loses them.

    In these situations the parent owns the problem, and it is up to the parent to take action to prevent such natural consequences from occurring or reoccurring. The actions that are recommended, again, are:

    ■ Problem prevention through discussion
    ■ Polite requests
    ■ "I" messages
    ■ Logical consequences
    ■ Family meetings

Logical Consequences

Because parents cannot always rely on natural consequences, and since prevention, polite requests and "I" messages are not always effective, logical consequences can be set up to handle parent-owned problems and to teach responsibility. We call them "logical" consequences because they are logically related to the child's misbehavior.

Born Again

Dennis The Menace ® used by permission of Hank Ketcham and © by North American Syndicate.

Logical consequences are those results a parent provides to teach children what logically follows when they violate family rules or the needs of a situation.

■ When Sean continues to forget to bring his dirty dishes into the kitchen after snacking in the den, he loses the privilege of taking food out of the kitchen.

■ When Dennis The Menace® (or Zack) uses crayon on the wall, he must use his time and energy to wash it off.

Logical Consequences Versus Punishment

Logical consequences are not the same thing as punishment, even though the child will usually experience both as unpleasant. Here are some of the differences:

Logical Consequences . . .

are logically connected to the misbehavior.

are intended to teach responsible behavior.

are administered in a firm and calm manner.

Punishment . . .

is an arbitrary retaliation for misbehavior.

is intended to teach blindly obedient behavior.

is often delivered in an atmosphere of anger and resentment.

Guidelines for Using Logical Consequences

1. Give the child a choice.

The consequences of children's choices teach them how to make better choices in the future

It is essential to give children choices regarding their behavior and the consequences of their behavior. As we have emphasized, learning how to handle responsibility is learning how to make choices. The consequences of children's choices teach them how to make better choices in the future. Parents can help children in this learning process by showing them that misbehavior (that is, a negative approach to their goals) is one of their choices, but that it brings with it logical consequences. It should also be emphasized to the child that the other choice, the positive approach to their goals, will bring about positive consequences.

There are two types of choices you will find extremely useful:

■ Either-or choices, usually phrased like this: "Either you may . . . or you may . . . You decide."

■ When-then choices, phrased like this: "When you have . . . then you may . . ."

Examples of Either-Or Choices

■ (Katherine leaves her belongings scattered around the kitchen in the afternoon.) "Katherine, either put your things away when you come home from school, or I'll put them in a box in the basement. You decide." (Notice that the logical consequence of leaving her belongings lying around is the inconvenience of having to dig them out of a junk box in the basement.)

■ (Calvin continues to forget to put his dirty clothes in the hamper.) "Calvin, either put your dirty clothes in the hamper, or wash them yourself. You decide." (The logical consequence of not putting his dirty clothes in the hamper is that he must do his own wash . . . or wear dirty clothes.)

Examples of When-Then Choices

■ (Maria has trouble getting her homework done but likes to spend time watching TV.) "Maria, when you have finished your homework, then you may turn on the TV." (Notice that the logical consequence of not doing her homework is losing the privilege of watching TV.)

■ (Tom is about to leave for the basketball court, ignoring his regular Saturday chore of mopping the kitchen.) "Tom, when you have mopped the kitchen, then you may go play basketball."

Here are some poorly expressed choices. The following examples are poorly expressed because they are couched in negative terms: "Don't do that or else . . ." They sound like punishment.

- ■ **Poor:** "Katherine, put your things away or I'm going to throw them in a box in the basement!"

- ■ **Poor:** "Calvin, if you don't start putting you dirty clothes in the hamper, you're going to have to wash them yourself."

- ■ **Poor:** "Tom, you may not go play basketball until you have mopped the kitchen."

2. Ask the child to help set the consequences.

Remember, life in our democratic society requires the participation of all those concerned with a problem. We stand a much better chance that the child will cooperate with our authority if we include her in the decision-making process. In addition, you'll be surprised how often the child will come up with choices and solutions that we wouldn't have thought of alone. For example:

"Katherine, I still have a problem with your leaving your belongings all over the kitchen. What do you think we can do to solve it?"

Even if the child has no helpful suggestions or is uncooperative about finding a solution, the important thing is that you asked. Since you have invited the child's participation, she will be less likely to think of you as a dictator and to rebel against you. (You will want to come to the discussion prepared with your own logical consequences in case the child has no ideas.)

3. Make sure the consequences are really logical.

One key to the success of logical consequences is that the consequence is logically connected to the misbehavior. Children are better able to see the justice of such consequences and will usually accept them without resentment. However, if the consequence you select is not really related to the child's behavior, it will come across as a punishment.

Not Logical	Logical
"Either come in to dinner when I call or no TV for a week."	"Either come in to dinner when I call or it will get cold—and you may miss it altogether."
"Either play quietly while I work or I'm not taking you to the movie we planned."	"When it gets quiet enough for me to finish my work, then I'll continue so that we'll be able to make the movie."
"Either stop fighting or you'll both get a spanking."	"Either stop fighting or you'll have to play in separate rooms."

4. Only give choices you can live with.

There are many potential logical consequences for any given problem. For that reason, brainstorming with other parents, a spouse, or even the child can help. However, when you own the problem, it is up to you to decide which choices to give your child. Only give choices you as a parent can accept.

For example, if your child continues to forget to put his dishes in the dishwasher, a choice might be:

"Either put your dishes in the dishwasher, or I'll leave them in the sink and there will be no clean dishes."

However, if you know a sink of dirty dishes will drive you crazy, then don't give him this choice. Why? Because you will likely sabotage the consequences by getting angry at him as the dishes pile up. In addition, your own values and likes are important. It is much better to keep thinking until you can come up with a consequence that won't punish you. For example:

"Either put your dirty dishes in the dishwasher, or I will serve the next meal without dishes."

By the way, parents who have used the above consequence say it takes only one meal of spaghetti eaten off a bare table by hand to teach the lesson. However, once again, if you couldn't live with the mess, then don't give this particular choice. What works for one family may not be acceptable for another.

5. Keep your tone firm and calm.

When giving the choice, as well as later when you enforce the consequence, it is essential that you remain both firm and calm. An angry tone of voice (the autocratic parent's pitfall) invites rebellion and a fight. On the other hand, a wishy-washy tone of voice (the permissive parent's pitfall) suggests to the child that you don't really mean what you say, and it also invites rebellion. In a democratic society, a firm and calm tone used by an authority figure says, "Hey, I recognize that we are equals and I will treat you respectfully, but you are out-of-bounds here. My job is to help you learn to stay in bounds, and I plan to do my job."

6. Give the choice one time, then act.

For a logical consequence to teach a lesson, it must be enforced. If the child continues to choose the negative approach (the misbehavior), then immediately follow through with the consequences. Children always choose. Even if they don't respond verbally, their behavior will tell you what choice has been made. Do not give the choice a second time without putting the consequences into effect. The child must see that the choice results in a consequence, and the lesson must be clear, or the value is diminished. For example:

Children don't do what doesn't work.

"If your books were in the kitchen when I cleaned, then you will find them in the junk box in the basement."

7. Expect testing.

When you attempt to redirect a child's misbehavior from negative choices towards positive ones, expect her to continue to misbehave for a while. We call this testing, because the child is actually testing to see if we will really do what we say we will do. In other words, will we change our behavior? For better or for worse, she was getting some pay-off out of our old way of responding, and she will try to get us to go back to that familiar parent-child cycle. However, if we will consistently enforce the consequences, she will soon see that her testing isn't working and change. After all, children don't do what doesn't work.

8. Allow the child to try again after experiencing the consequences.

Since the goal is for the child to learn from the consequences of his choice, opportunities must be provided to try again—but only after the child has experienced the consequences of the first choice. For example, Tom has agreed that when he has mopped the kitchen, then he may go play basketball on Saturdays. Dad sees Tom heading to the courts before the kitchen is mopped and reminds him of his obligation.

If the child repeats the misbehavior after experiencing the consequences, then he is testing. One can meet this challenge by letting the consequences operate a little longer after the second try, and longer yet after the third. For example, if Tom starts for the basketball court again next week without doing his chores, Dad can say,

"It seems that you have decided not to play ball today. We can try again next week."

Logical Consequences Guidelines

1. Give the child a choice.
   - ■ either/or choice
   - ■ when/then choice

2. Ask the child to help.

3. Make sure the consequence is logical.

4. Give choices you can live with.

5. Keep your tone firm and calm.

6. Give the choice one time, then act.

7. Expect testing.

8. Allow the child to try again later.

Mutual Respect

Respect is an important aspect of all relationships in a society based on equality. Its absence erodes the possibility of cooperation, and breeds resentment and hostility. Teaching children respect is therefore an important goal of *Active Parenting Today*. How do we teach this basic skill? The best way to teach respect is to show respect. When we treat our children respectfully, then we are on firm ground when we expect them to treat us the same. This concept of "mutual respect" between parent and child is an idea many parents have found invaluable.

The best way to teach respect is to show respect.

Most adults have learned how to show respect towards other adults. Yet it is easy for parents to slip into disrespect when addressing their own children. Parents humiliate, criticize, nag, belittle, remind, yell, label, name-call and intimidate; parents do for children what children could do for themselves; parents put themselves in service to their children and even allow children to abuse them (these too are disrespectful); parents don't listen when children talk, but become furious when children do the same thing to them. The list goes on.

As you apply the discipline skills from this session, work at catching yourself before you act disrespectfully to your children. Try to catch yourself with a smile, rather than a kick, and then look for a way to express yourself that is consistent with how you would like to be treated. Notice how your child responds, and how you feel during the exchange.

Family Enrichment Activity
Positive "I" Messages

As we have seen earlier in this chapter, "I" messages offer parents an effective way to confront their children about repeated misbehavior. They are clear, firm, calm communications that are often easy for children to hear without becoming defensive. These same features also make it possible to use "I" messages as encouraging statements when children are behaving well. Positive "I" messages, as we call them, can help motivate a child to continue improving her behavior.

For example, in one of the video vignettes, Laura uses a logical consequence to teach her son Zack not to draw handprints on the wall. She then follows up with a positive "I" message. Let's see how one is constructed:

1. **State what you like.** *"I really like the way you are using paper for your art project."*

2. **Say how you feel.** *"I feel good knowing that you heard what I said about the walls."*

3. **Tell them why.** *"Because now we can have clean walls and an artistic use of white space."*

4. **Offer to do something for them.** *"How about if we tape your picture over here like a painting in a museum?"*

This fourth step is new because when disciplining using "I" messages, we are telling the children what we want them to do. When we offer to do something for them, we want to make sure it doesn't become a reward. It will help to keep the offer logically connected to their positive behavior. You might even think of this as a "positive logical consequence." For example:

■ After using "I" messages and logical consequences to decrease the fighting between your children, you catch them cooperating. At the end of your positive "I" message, you let them know that their cooperation has let you get your work done faster so now you have time to make some popcorn, play with them, or teach them how to play a new game.

Don't worry if you don't use every step of the positive "I" message every time. The first statement alone (telling them what you like) is a good use of encouragement by itself. And feel free to use your own words so that the message feels natural to you.

For your home activity, use the guide on the following page to develop a positive "I" message you might use at home this week. Plan it around the problem that you will be using the discipline "I" message or logical consequence to change.

Family Enrichment Activity

Positive "I" Messages

I like _____

I feel _____

Because _____

How about if I _____

Afterwards,

What did you like about how it went? _____

_____

What will you do differently next time?_____

_____

_____

_____

_____

_____

_____

_____

_____

_____

_____

_____

Who Owns the Problem Video Practice

Scene 1. (Laura and Zack - phone.)

Who owns the problem? _____

Why? _____

_____

Scene 2. (Laura and Zack - shoes.)

Who owns the problem? _____

Why? _____

_____

Scene 3. (Kathi and Jade - swing.)

Who owns the problem? _____

Why? _____

_____

Scene 4. (José, Ramon and Sara - kicking.)

Who owns the problem? _____

Why ? _____

_____

Scene 5. (Think of a problem from your own family.)

What is the problem?_____

Who owns the problem? _____

Why?_____

_____

"I" Messages

Try writing an "I" message for the following example: Your 10-year-old son has been playing loudly for the past 15 minutes and you're getting a terrible headache. You've already asked him politely to play quietly, but somehow he has gotten loud again. Fill in the following "I" message as you might express it to your son:

I have a problem with _____

I feel _____

because _____

I would like (Will you please) _____

Write down a problem from your own family in which you own the problem. _____

Now write an "I" message that you can use at home this week to solve the problem: _____

When _____

I feel _____

because _____

I would like (Will you please) _____

Evaluation

How did your child respond to your "I" message? _____

What did you like about the way you delivered the "I" message? _____

How would you do it differently next time? _____

Logical Consequences Video Practice

Scene	Guideline Violated	Possible Logical Consequences
Scene 1. Ramon oversleeping		
Scene 2. Ramon oversleeping		
Scene 3. Janelle skating in street		
Scene 4. Ben not eating his peas		
Scene 5. Jade not returning art supplies		

Using Logical Consequences

Think of a problem you would like to solve using a logical consequence. (You may choose the same problem for which you constructed an "I" message on page 112 as a back-up in case the "I" message is not effective.) Write in the space below one way that you might present the choices and consequences to your child during the discussion of the problem. _____

_____

_____

Meet with your child to discuss the problem, and use this logical consequence or one that you develop with the child.

Evaluation

What was your child's response to the discussion?_____

_____

_____

What was his response to the logical consequence? (Did he test you to see if you would follow through?)

_____

_____

If the consequence isn't working, do you think you need to stick with it longer or change the consequence to something else? _____

_____

_____

If the consequence isn't working, have you violated any of the guidelines for setting up logical consequences? (Check page 106.)

What do you like about the way you handled the use of logical consequences? _____

_____

What will you do differently next time?_____

Chapter Four. Home Activities Checklist

(Check when completed.)

❑ 1. Read Chapter Four. If you would like to read ahead, please do so.

❑ 2. Practice the Family Enrichment Activity: Positive "I" Messages on page 110.

❑ 3. Try an "I" message, and fill in the guide sheet on page 112.

❑ 4. Talk about your problem with your child and apply a logical consequence (complete page 114).

❑ 5. Be aware of speaking respectfully to your children.

❑ 6. Call your buddy (optional).

Notes

Winning
Cooperation

An oarsman on a Roman galley was rowing to the beat of the drum. He looked over at the oarsman next to him and was horrified at what he saw. The oarsman in the next seat was drilling a hole in the bottom of the boat under his seat. As the water began to gush into the boat, the first oarsman exclaimed, "What in Jupiter's name are you doing?" The man replied, "What's it to you? I'm only drilling the hole under *my* seat."

The joke, of course, is that when we are all riding in the same boat, no matter whose seat the hole is under, everyone is going to get wet. Nowhere is this more true than in a family. When one member has a problem, the ripples are felt throughout the family.

Active Parenting Today has stressed four main qualities that form the foundation of the individual's ability to succeed in our democratic society: courage, self-esteem, responsibility and cooperation. Cooperation, the gentle art of working together for the common good, is the subject of this chapter.

Communication: The Road to Cooperation

Families and societies that recognize we are all traveling in the same boat place a tremendous value on cooperation. They know that people will perform better when they have the ability to participate in the decision-making process. They understand that none of us is as smart and as capable as all of us. They see that when people work together cooperatively, amazing things happen—problems are solved and civilizations are built.

Cooperation is two or more people working together in a mutually supportive manner toward a common goal.

In a society of equals, the child who learns to work cooperatively with others, to be a team player, has a far greater chance of success than the one who overemphasizes competition. Ironically, though the ability to compete is certainly a major part of our society, the ability to cooperate is what makes us great.

One of the best ways to teach cooperation to your child is through problem solving. In the last chapter we discussed the role of discipline in handling problems that belong to the parent. Even with parent-owned problems, we stressed the importance of including the child in the problem-solving process. In those cases when the problem belongs to the child, we have a unique opportunity to *help* the child find a solution. We can do this respectfully, without robbing the child of the responsibility for handling his problem. We can do this with good communication skills.

When we solve problems cooperatively, better solutions are found.

Through active communication between you and your child, an important side effect occurs: the child learns that "two heads are better than one"—that when we solve problems cooperatively, better solutions are found. This teamwork, and the solutions it often brings, not only fosters a respect for cooperation, it also strengthens the relationship between parent and child. And that translates to more satisfaction and harmony for the entire family.

The Problem-Handling Model

Let's look once again at the model for handling problems in a family. When we presented this model in Chapter Four, we focused on the discipline side of parenting (when we own the problem). Now we will look at the support side of parenting (when our child owns a problem). The skills used for supporting a child in solving a problem are highlighted in blue.

The Problem-Handling Model

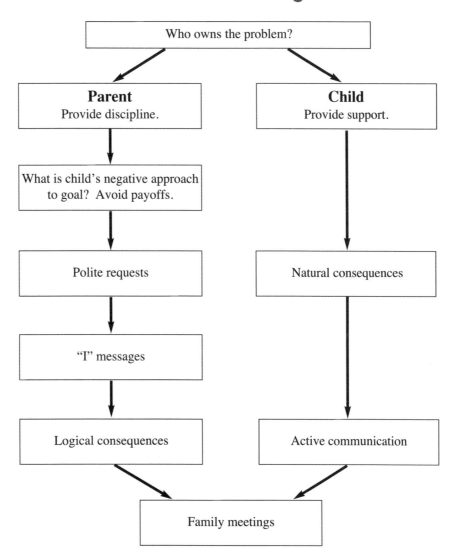

ENCOURAGE . . . ENCOURAGE . . . ENCOURAGE.

Avoiding Communication Blocks

Half of good communication is avoiding bad communication. When a child has a problem, she is particularly sensitive. If she pays us the great compliment of beginning to discuss this problem with us, she is putting her self-esteem at risk. If we say or do something that injures her self-esteem at this point, she will withdraw. In other words, we will have blocked the communication.

> *A communication block is any remark or attitude on the part of the listener that injures the speaker's self-esteem to the extent that communication is broken off.*

For example, a child is sharing his outrage. Never mind whether the outrage is ugly or not; never mind whether the child is "right" or not. The parent can choose to listen to the content of the outrage, or the parent can decide to keep things under control by commanding: "Don't talk back to me," or "Stop complaining." Further communication has been effectively blocked.

For example, a child is sharing her fear about an upcoming test of her courage or ability. The parent can listen to the content of that fear and allow the child to express as much of it as possible, or the parent can try to talk the child out of her feelings by placating or distracting: "You usually come through okay." "It isn't really as bad as it seems." "Let's not worry about that; things will look brighter tomorrow." Why should a child continue sharing her fears with someone who says they are insignificant? Communication is blocked.

For example, a child is sharing his pain surrounding difficulties with enemies or friends or teachers or family members. The parent can listen to the content of that pain, or the parent can moralize or play psychologist: "You're just jealous, that's all." "You should know better than to act that way." "You brought all this on yourself, you know."

The parents who construct these communication blocks usually do so with good intentions:

- The parent who commands wants to keep things under control.

- The parent who gives advice wants to influence the child with arguments or opinions.

- The parent who placates or distracts with sweet words wants to protect the child from the problem, and so tries to get the child to think of something else.

- The parent who plays psychologist wants to analyze the child's behavior and explain the child's motives.

- The parent who moralizes wants the child to deal with the problem in a way that the parent thinks is proper.

- The parent who uses sarcasm feels that by making the child feel silly or ridiculous, the child will see how wrong her attitudes and behavior are.

- The parent who acts like a know-it-all believes his greater experience gives him the right and/or duty to give the child the correct answers.

None of these parents is listening to the child! All of these parents block further communication by the things they say.

Communication blocks are usually a product of disrespect. It is not that we mean the child any harm; in fact, our intentions are usually to help. However, our attitude demeans the child in some way. In our society of equals, an individual's self-esteem is very important. We are wary of signs of disrespect, and we are quick to withdraw from those who show us these signs. Yet we all make these mistakes and block communication. Please look at the chart of common communication blocks on the following page, and try to recognize which ones you use most often.

When active communication skills are used, the child feels comfortable going to the parent with problems.

When a child runs into communication blocks often enough, the child eventually decides that this is not a person to trust with a problem. On the positive side, when active communication skills are used, the child feels comfortable going to the parent with problems, even big ones. The parent then becomes what is sometimes called an "askable parent"—someone whose opinion the child will *ask* for. Later, when it comes to critical matters such as sexuality, tobacco, alcohol and other drugs, it pays to have established such an open line of communication.

121

Communication Blocks

Communication block	Parent's intention	Why it's disrespectful	Examples
Commanding	To control the situation and provide child with quick solutions.	It says to the child, "You don't have the right to decide how to handle your own problems."	"What you should do is . . ." "Stop complaining."
Giving Advice	To influence the child with arguments or opinions.	It says to the child, "You don't have the good sense to come up with your own solutions."	"I've got a good idea . . ." "Why don't you . . ."
Placating	To take away the child's pain; to make her feel better.	It says to the child, "You don't have a right to your feelings; you can't handle discomfort."	"It isn't as bad as it seems." "Everything will be okay."
Interrogating	To get to the bottom of the problem and find out what the child did wrong.	It says to the child, "You must have messed up somewhere."	"What did you do to him . . ."
Distracting	To protect the child from the problem by changing the subject.	It says to the child, "I don't think you can stand the discomfort long enough to find a real solution."	"Let's not worry about that, let's . . ."
Psychologizing	To help prevent future problems by analyzing the child's behavior and explaining his motives.	It says to the child, "I know more about you than you know about yourself. Therefore, I'm superior to you."	"Do you know why you said that?" "You're just insecure."
Sarcasm	To show the child how wrong her attitudes or behavior are by making her feel ridiculous.	It says to the child, "You are ridiculous."	"Well, I guess that's just about the end of the world."
Moralizing	To show the child the proper way to deal with the problem.	It says to the child, "Don't you dare choose your own values."	"The right thing to do would be to . . ." "Oh, how awful."
Know-It-All	To show the child that he has a resource for handling any problem; namely, the parent.	It says to the child, "Since I know it all, you must know nothing."	"The solution is really very simple."

More of the message is
delivered by tone of
voice, and most by our
body language,
including facial
expressions.

Mixed Messages

What we communicate to our children will spring from our attitudes and values—our thinking. *How* these messages are delivered has to do with three channels of communication: words, tone of voice and body language. As surprising as it may seem, a small fraction of our communication is carried by the words themselves. More of the message is delivered by tone of voice, and most by our body language, including facial expressions.

When all three channels are carrying the same message, the communication is clear and can be very powerful. However, when we are saying one thing with our words but something quite different with our tone and/or body language, we send what is called a "mixed message." This can be confusing to a child.

For example, your child owns a problem and you have decided to let her handle it. Your child thinks you might be angry if she decides to do what she wants rather than what you think is best.

Your words say: "I'm not angry. You can do whatever you like." But your face and tone say: "I'll be very angry if you don't do what I think is best." This sort of mixed message blocks communication and makes it difficult for your child to know where she really stands. If your child owns a problem, you may need to adjust your attitude so that you really accept her right to make the decision without your anger. You may still be somewhat disappointed, but you can change your words to be more consistent. For example:

"I may be disappointed if you decide not to take your sister with you to the playground, but as I said, it's your choice, and I can live with it."

When a parent owns the problem and discipline is used, mixed messages only serve to blur the limits and invite children to hear the channel they want to hear.

For example, your child asks if he can stay up an extra hour to watch a TV program.

Your words say one thing: "I don't think that's a very good idea."

But your tone says something different: "I'm not really

that concerned, and if you go ahead and stay up anyway, you probably won't get in trouble."

What do you think your child will do? Since more of the message is carried through tone of voice, he's probably going to stay up. An important principle of communication is this: *Clarity leads to power*.

The clearer we are about what we want from our children, where the limits are, and when we are willing to back off and let them make decisions for themselves, the more powerful an influence we will become. And the more powerful people they will become.

Active Communication

Active communication is a set of communication skills that allows a parent to support a child in handling her own problems. These skills can be learned, and they can be steadily improved with practice. Active communication is called for in situations in which the child owns the problem, or in which the child and the parent share responsibility for the problem. There are five skills involved:

1. Listen actively.
2. Listen for feelings.
3. Connect feelings to content.
4. Look for alternatives and evaluate consequences.
5. Follow up.

1. Listen actively.

Keeping in mind the need to avoid communication blocks, let's move to the first step in active communication: active listening. Why do we say "active" listening? Because if you listen fully, you are not just a passive receiver of information; you are an active participant in the communication process. You listen with your eyes as well as your ears, with your intuition as well as your thinking ability. Your object in listening actively is to encourage the child to express what he is thinking and feeling. Here is how:

- **Keep your own talk to a minimum.** You are not listening when you are talking. When you are actively listening to a child, your role is to listen, not talk.

- **Give full attention.** When parents are listening actively, they give their full attention to the child and what he is saying. When parents give their full attention, the child will usually feel encouraged by the attention alone. The attention says, "I care about you; you matter; I'm here to help."

- **Acknowledge what you are hearing.** Active listening is not characterized by absolute silence on the part of the listener. When listening to a child, it helps to show that you are understanding, that you are taking it in. You can say something as simple as "I see" now and then, or even "Umm-hmm." You can ask questions that clarify what the child is saying, or you can summarize lengthy or complicated stories.

Empathy is the art of sharing another person's feelings.

- **Listen with empathy.** Empathy is the art of sharing another person's feelings. Allow yourself to feel some of what your child is feeling, and indicate through tone of voice and facial expression that you are experiencing the impact of what is being said. In short, you are listening to the feelings beneath the words your child is saying.

2. Listen for feelings.

There are no wrong feelings, for either parents or children. There are certainly unpleasant feelings, and they often suggest mistaken attitudes or beliefs, but feelings in themselves are not wrong or right. They simply are, and whether we like it or not, they influence us. In fact, they influence us more when we don't acknowledge and accept them. Acknowledging and accepting our feelings doesn't necessarily mean we act on them. Instead, we want to help children learn to pause and reflect on their feelings *before* deciding what action to take.

The parent will have to listen closely to tone of voice and observe facial expressions to hear what the child is feeling.

So, acknowledging our feelings surrounding a problem is often a first step in dealing with that problem. Parents can help children learn to acknowledge their feelings by listening for the feelings the child experiences, not just the content of the story. Until a child has been taught to describe her feelings with words, the parent will have to listen closely to tone of voice and observe facial expressions to "hear" what the child is feeling.

As we teach our children to name their feelings, we help them to better express unpleasant feelings in words rather than act them out in misbehavior or express them physically through stomachaches, headaches or other stress related problems. Finally, when we listen with empathy for the feelings behind the child's story, we communicate the most powerful message of all: we care. An important principle of helping is this:

> *No one cares how much you know until they know how much you care.*

Take time to hear your child's feelings, and your caring will open the door to communication and problem solving.

3. Connect feelings to content.

When a parent has actively listened to the content of what a child has to say, and has an idea of what the child is feeling, the next step is to reflect those feelings back to the child. The parent becomes what psychologist Haim Ginott calls an "emotional mirror." Just as it isn't the job of the mirror to pass judgment about how we look or tell us what to do, the job of the parent is only to reflect the feelings of the child and connect them to what happened—the "content." This "reflection" takes the form of a tentative statement like this:

"It sounds as though you are sad that Lonnie can't come over today."

"I guess you were angry when she said that."

By reflecting feelings in tentative terms—for example, "It sounds as though . . ." or "I guess . . ."—we don't come across as a mind reader or know-it-all. And if we miss our guess as to what the child is feeling, she can comfortably correct us. For example:

"Not really. It's just so boring without anyone to play with."

"Maybe a little angry, but mostly it hurt my feelings."

The parent can then simply say, "Oh, I see; you felt hurt," and the communication continues to flow.

When we reflect the feeling accurately, an exciting thing happens. The child nods her head in recognition, often says "yes," and then continues to share. She feels understood and cared for—and she understands herself a little better. The communication path is now clearer and she is closer to finding an effective solution.

What the Child Says	Feeling Word	What the Parent Can Say
Mom, I'm not going to clean up my dumb room!	Angry	You're angry that I want you to clean up your room.
I missed the foul shot, and we lost the game.	Disappointed	Sounds like you're disappointed about missing the shot.
I hate the way I look in this hat.	Embarrassed	You're embarrassed to wear that hat.

4. Look for alternatives and evaluate consequences.

Helping a child become an effective problem solver means helping him look at alternative solutions and weigh the potential consequences. Many times, merely helping the child to connect feeling and content is enough to suggest a solution. However, some problems are more difficult to deal with than others, and they require some action to remedy the situation. In many cases a parent can begin by encouraging the child to look at the possible alternatives:

"What can you do about that?"

"What else can you try?"

After each alternative, the parent can help the child predict the consequences of that alternative:

"What do you think would happen if you did that?"

It is better for the child to think of alternatives on her own, without prompting. If the child cannot think of any, the parent can tentatively suggest some. Also, it can be helpful for a parent to share a personal experience in a similar situation, so long as she doesn't use the testimonial as a weapon, to urge the child toward a specific course of action. Instead, you could say something like this:

"I don't know what you will decide to do, but I remember a time when a friend of mine named Anita moved away without even saying good-bye. I felt hurt, then angry, then sad."

It is important to let the child have final responsibility for deciding which alternative she will choose. Refrain from telling the child what to do. The choice must be the child's if she is to learn responsibility. When a child figures out what to do, she feels a sense of self-esteem and accepts responsibility for her choices.

You're out to empower him, not control him.

Your position during this discussion should be what we call "palms up." A palms up gesture says to your child, "I don't know what you will decide to do; the decision is in *your* hands." By actually turning your palms up while saying, "I don't know what you will decide to do," you present a supportive, non-threatening ally to the child, one who invites cooperation. Contrast this with the finger-pointing position of the dictator who says, "Here's what you need to do," and you can see how the palms up approach actually increases your ability to influence your child's decisions. After all, why shouldn't he listen to your alternatives? You're out to empower him, not control him.

5. Follow up.

Before ending the discussion, it is often helpful to ask the child what he intends to do, and when. This can be done gently, with an understanding that even Einstein often needed some time to think about new information before his course of action became clear.

Follow up by asking the child how the solution turned out.

After the child has had an opportunity to handle the problem, follow up by asking the child how the solution turned out.

"How did it go with . . ."

In doing so, the parent not only helps the child make sense of the total experience, but also confirms to him that the interest was genuine. If the problem still exists, you can also move back into active communication.

Feeling Words

Although the English language has hundreds of words that describe specific feelings, most people do not have many in their daily vocabulary. As you practice looking for the right "feeling words," you will find your feeling word vocabulary increases and the job gets easier. To help with this process, we have included a list of 100 feeling words for you to keep in mind.

Words That Describe Pleasant Feelings

accepted	hopeful
adequate	honored
adventurous	important
bold	joyful
brilliant	lovely
calm	loving
caring	overjoyed
cheerful	peaceful
comfortable	peppy
confident	playful
content	pleased
daring	proud
eager	refreshed
elated	relieved
encouraged	satisfied
energetic	secure
excited	snappy
fascinated	successful
free	surprised
full	sympathetic
glad	tranquil
great	understood
gutsy	warm
happy	wonderful
high	zany

Words That Describe Unpleasant Feelings

afraid	jealous
angry	let down
anxious	lonely
ashamed	miserable
bashful	nervous
bored	overwhelmed
cautious	pained
cheated	possessive
concerned	provoked
defeated	pushed
defiant	rejected
disappointed	remorseful
discouraged	resentful
down	shy
embarrassed	stupid
envious	suspicious
foolish	tired
frustrated	trapped
guilty	uncomfortable
hateful	uneasy
hesitant	unhappy
hopeless	unloved
hurt	unsure
impatient	weary
irritated	worried

Putting Active Communication to Work

Now that you are aware of the five steps of the active communication process, begin looking for opportunities to use them in helping your child find solutions to problems. You'll find that the more supportive you are, the more cooperative your child is likely to become.

However, if your relationship is still characterized by power struggles, disrespect and anger, then your child may not be willing yet to sit down for a lengthy discussion. You can still use what you have learned to begin winning his cooperation by listening for his feelings and expressing empathy. For example:

"Boy, you sure look down."

"I guess you're really ticked off."

"That must have really hurt."

You can even use this skill when disciplining your child or denying him permission to do something. It may help reduce his anger. Just having his feelings recognized and accepted can sometimes help. For example:

"I know you're angry that I won't let you go."

"If looks could kill, I'd be in real trouble right now."

"I can live with you hating me right now, but I don't think I could live with hating myself if I let you do something I knew was dangerous, and something terrible happened to you."

The following scene from the *Active Parenting Today* video offers a good example of the entire active communication process in action. See if you can identify where the five steps are used:

Janelle: I don't believe it!

Pat: You don't believe what?

Janelle: Mrs. Hickman. I was sitting there minding my own business while Denise and Cathy keep whispering to me about this birthday party and I told them I was going but to please be quiet. Then Mrs. Hickman looks up and sees me whispering to Denise to be quiet and thinks I'm the one who was talking and gave me extra homework because I 'apparently have so much time on my hands that I don't know what to do.' It isn't fair.

Pat: You sure sound angry.

Janelle: Yes. Wouldn't you? I mean, I didn't even want to be talking!

Pat: And yet you're the one who got in trouble. I can see why you'd be upset.

Janelle: And to make matters worse, Denise and Cathy didn't say a word. They just sat there and giggled.

Pat: You must have been furious about that.

Janelle: I'll say! They started it, and then let me take all the blame!

Pat: And, of course, all Mrs. Hickman saw was you talking.

Janelle: Right. So she thinks it's all my fault.

Pat: I guess you were a little embarrassed, too, when she called you down in front of the whole class.

Janelle: Yeah. But the other kids saw what was going on, so it wasn't that bad. But now I have all this homework to do. Well, it's not fair. I'm not going to do it.

Pat: That's one thing you could do. What would happen if you didn't do it?

Janelle: I guess she'd give me an "F" to average in with my grades.

Pat: Ouch! That could really hurt, especially after all the hard work you've put in. What else could you do?

Janelle: I could tell what really happened?

Pat: Yes, you could. What do you think would happen then?

Janelle: Well, the other kids would probably put me down for being a tattletale, and Mrs. Hickman would just tell me I had no business talking anyway—that I should have ignored them.

Pat: What do you think about that?

Janelle: I guess it was pretty dumb. I mean, I guess I knew that she doesn't allow talking and all, but Mom, I didn't want them to think I'm a snob.

Pat: I see. You're afraid they wouldn't like you if you had followed Mrs. Hickman's rules and kept quiet. So you let them get you in trouble because you want them to like you.

Janelle: Yeah. Pretty dumb, wasn't it?

Pat: Well . . . let's put it this way: It's only dumb if you keep doing it. It may be a mistake that you can learn something from.

(Pat and Janelle in the kitchen a few days later.)

Pat: Oh, Janelle. I've been meaning to ask—How did that whispering in class thing work out? Did you do the extra homework?

Janelle: Yeah. I didn't think an "F" would be too great.

Pat: And how about Denise and Cathy? They still getting you to talk during class?

Janelle: No way! I told them I didn't like what they did, and that the next time I was just going to ignore them.

Pat: Attagirl. I like the way you stood up for yourself. It's smart to not let people take advantage of you.

Family Enrichment Activity

Bedtime Routines and I Love You's

Children, particularly young children, want and need a certain amount of structure in their days. Knowing that certain things happen at certain times and in certain ways offers a sense of security and order to their worlds. As they get older, they can develop their own structures, and can depend on us less.

As with most things, moderation is still a key. A rigid structure that can never vary is just as bad as a structure that is so flexible children never know what they can count on.

One of the best structures you can develop for your children is a bedtime routine. Although many parents experience conflict at bedtime, it doesn't have to be that way. Like many of the problems that have been discussed in this program, we can use the prevention ideas described in Chapter Four to turn bedtime into a positive time of day. Particularly remember:

1. Make it a win/win for both of you.
You can help make the bedtime routine more acceptable to your children if you look for ways to involve them in the process and to make it fun.

2. Encourage . . . encourage . . . encourage.
Bedtime can be one of the happiest times of the day for both you and your children if you make it fun and involving. Here is one good routine that has been successful in many families with young children:

- Begin with bath time. Bath time can easily be experienced as a continuation of play time for the kids when you add a little music, some bathtub toys and make it fun for yourself, too. For example:

"Here's the world famous diver getting ready to do a triple somersault into a tub of wet children."

- Teeth brushing. Bath time, of course, is followed by teeth brushing, which may never qualify as fun, but getting your children involved and using some encouragement can at least keep them on the right track. For example:

"You're doing such a good job. I really appreciate the way you're keeping your mouth open. Can you open as wide as a lion?"

- Bedtime story. One of the favorite bedtime routines is a bedtime story. Whether it be a book or a made-up story, this offers a pleasant transition from the active play of the day to the quiet of bedtime. With older children you might substitute some quiet talk about the events of the day instead of a story. Whatever you do during this "talk and touch time," it's an opportunity for winding down and relaxing.

- Special rituals. Then it's time for lights out and your own special rituals. This might include a prayer if you like, and then other regular words or actions—a back rub, a special poem or something you make up. For example:

"If all the little girls in the whole wide world were put end to end and I could choose anyone to be my daughter, I'd choose you."

- Expressing love. Building a positive relationship with children is an ongoing process, and it sometimes takes steady effort. As we have seen, it involves making arrangements to have fun together, teaching specific skills to children, and mutual respect. But the positive relationship between parent and child involves, most of all, expressing love for each other. All children hunger for love, even those who make a career of acting "unlovable." Children need to know that whatever else may happen, their parents love them. Methods of expressing love to children can be woven into the fabric of everyday life: a kiss, a pat on the back, a tousling of hair, an arm around the shoulder. But it is equally important to be able to say to your child that you love him. The words may come awkwardly for some parents. But the important thing is how beautiful they sound to children.

Parents can say "I love you" when the child will be surprised at the timing, but pleased with the message. Parents can say "I love you" at a time of calmness or tenderness, such as bedtime, and the child can bask in the warmth of the words. For example:

"I love you."

Family Enrichment Activity
Bedtime Routines and I Love You's

Remember when . . .
Think back once again to when you were a child, and recall what bedtime was like in your family. Was there a set routine? Was it a positive time for closeness? Were there "I love you's"?

Describe the usual routine: _____

_____

How did you think and feel? _____

_____

What is your routine with your children? _____

_____

How might you improve it? _____

_____

After you have had a chance to put your changes into practice, jot down how it went for you and your child:

_____

Expressing Love at Home
Bedtime can be a special time to express love to your children. There are many other opportunities as well. To help you remember your expressions of love to your children, fill in the following chart:

Child's Name	Your Expression	Your Child's Reaction

Communication Blocks Activity

We all use communication blocks at one time or another. Or, as one parent put it, "My skill is such that I can use three or four of these blocks at one time." To catch ourselves before we block communication, it helps to know what our individual pitfalls are.

Think about the communication blocks you tend to use most often. Write them under "block" below. Then indicate the situations that usually bring them out, and what you see as your intention for using each block.

Block	Situation	Intention
Example: *Distracting*	*Son didn't get the part in the school play.*	*To make him feel better so I'd feel better.*

Active Communication Evaluation

After you've had a chance to practice your active communication skills with one of your children this week, fill out the following evaluation so that you can be sure to learn from the experience.

What was the situation or problem that you talked to your child about? _____

_____

_____

How did you approach your child? _____

_____

_____

List examples of the five steps of active communication you were able to use:

1. Listen actively _____

2. Listen for feelings _____

3. Connect feelings to content _____

4. Look for alternatives and evaluate consequences _____

5. Follow up _____

How did your child respond to your effort? _____

_____

What did you like about how you handled the process? _____

_____

What would you do differently next time? _____

_____

Responding to Feelings Video Practice

Scene	Child's Feeling	Parent's Response
#1. Sara		
#2. Zack		
#3. Ramon		
#4. Ben		
#5. Jade		
#6. Janelle		
#7. Sara		
#8. Zack		
#9. Ramon		
#10. Jade		

Chapter Five. Home Activities Checklist

(Check when completed.)

❑ 1. Read Chapter Five. If you wish to read ahead, please do so.

❑ 2. Do the Family Enrichment Activity: Bedtime Routines and I Love You's on page 135.

❑ 3. Look for at least one opportunity to use active communication when your child owns a problem, and fill in the guide sheet on page 137.

❑ 4. Call your buddy and encourage each other (optional).

Notes

Active Parenting in a Democratic Society

There was a television show a number of years ago that began with the words, "Democracy is a very bad form of government . . . but all of the others are so much worse." Well, we don't believe democracy is really a bad form of government, just an imperfect one. It does have its problems, but with a cooperative and responsible effort on the part of its citizens (backed with a collective profile of courage), it can work splendidly. And it is up to each of us to make it work.

Because the purpose of *Active Parenting Today* is to support you in instilling in your children qualities that will enable them to survive and thrive in a democracy, what better place to begin teaching democratic principles than in the family?

But what are the principles of a democracy? See if you agree with our understanding of the democratic process:

Principles of Democracy

Principles	In a Democratic Society			In an Active Parenting Family		
	Yes	No	Comments	Yes	No	Comments
Equality is a prized value.	✔		"All . . . are created equal." The Declaration of Independence by Thomas Jefferson.	✔		Remember . . . "equal" does not mean "the same."
Citizens are free to do whatever they please.		✔	There are limits to freedom and consequences for breaking the laws set by the leaders . . . even for the leaders (that's equality again).		✔	Again, there is "freedom within expanding limits." Even parents must accept some limits and abide by consequences.
All citizens vote on everything.		✔	The elected leaders do most of the decision making.		✔	Parents are the leaders and they, too, must make most decisions.
All citizens have a voice and can influence the decisions of their leaders.	✔		Most elected leaders are highly sensitive to the opinions of their constituents.	✔		Active parents listen to the opinions of their children, and allow them to influence family decisions.
Everyone can vote for the leaders.		✔	Only adults vote. Only citizens vote.		✔	There are no voting booths in the womb. Children do not choose their parents.

Freedom of Speech

One of the themes stressed in *Active Parenting Today* is the importance of allowing children a voice in decisions that affect their lives. Just as freedom of speech is the basic freedom in our democratic society, a cooperative household must allow its members the same freedom. Of course, democracy doesn't mean you will always get your way; it means you will always get your say. By allowing children to influence our decisions through respectful discussion, we are better able to maintain our parental authority.

The feeling on the part of children that their voices and opinions make a difference builds cooperation and responsibility, and at the same time it makes anger and rebellion less likely. This chapter will present three types of family discussion that will offer you and your children opportunities for communicating as a cooperative unit:

Family Talks

These are brief discussions that center around topics of interest to you and your children. The purpose of these talks is to share attitudes and values in a way that influences children to make positive decisions later on.

Problem-Solving Discussions

These talks center around problems that need to be solved for the benefit of individual family members or the family as a whole.

Family Council Meetings

These weekly meetings provide the family a regular opportunity to handle family problems, discuss issues that affect the family, make plans, and otherwise conduct much of the business of the family. They may incorporate family talks and problem-solving discussions.

Because talking together as a family is such an important part of thriving in a democratic society, we suggest you begin these activities as soon as your children are old enough. Whether you choose to begin with the less formal family talks and problem-solving discussions, or to plunge right in with the family council meeting, it's important you make the effort to begin. You'll be using many of the skills you are already learning from previous chapters in these talks, so you have the necessary foundation.

With so many children running away from home and so many marriages ending in divorce, it would be nice if there were one simple formula for keeping the family together. There isn't. But what might come closest is the following, although overstated, slogan:

When the family talks, nobody walks.

Four More Good Reasons for Holding Family Meetings

1. Cooperation: Regular family meetings teach each person in the family that all are in the same boat, all on board can share in steering the boat, and the best way to decide how and where to steer it is to share feelings and opinions until an agreement is reached.

2. Responsibility: The regular participation in family meetings teaches each person in the family to make the best choices she can make on behalf of the family. After all, everyone will have to live with the consequences once the choices are made.

3. Courage: Family meetings are laboratories for individual courage. Each family member learns how important it is to say what he really thinks and feels, even if it isn't shared by anybody else. Meetings also provide opportunities for sharing encouragement.

4. Self-esteem:
When children see their ideas valued and their participation welcomed, they think well of themselves. This self-esteem can carry over into other aspects of their lives.

How To Get Started With a Family Meeting

Parents are usually the ones to present the idea of having family meetings and to get the meetings started. Here are some points for parents to consider in setting up a family meeting.

- **Start with those who are willing to attend.** In some situations, a few family members are not ready to discuss matters in a family meeting, or they feel the idea is not a good one. But this doesn't mean the idea should be abandoned. Family meetings can still be held, if most family members agree on holding them. Those who do not attend the early meetings may decide to attend later when they see the advantages.

- **Who should attend family meetings?** Family meetings should include parents, children and anyone who lives with the family, such as grandparents, uncles or aunts. In other words, anyone who has a stake in decisions affecting the daily life of the family should be present.

- **Single parent households.** Families affected by separation or divorce can still hold family meetings, even though one parent will not be participating. In those cases it is important for the family to avoid discussing matters pertaining to the children's relationship with the absent parent. Those matters are owned by the children and the absent parent. Such problems should be handled by active communication, away from the family meeting.

- **Time and place.** Select a time and a place convenient and agreeable to everyone who will be attending. A good time for family meetings is Sunday afternoons, the beginning of the week. The family is more likely to be together at that time, and the past week can be reviewed, the upcoming week anticipated. The meetings should be held in a place comfortable for all participants, preferably around a table with enough room for everyone to pull up a chair.

Family Talks

Family talks are discussions that focus on specific topics of interest or importance to family members. For example, honesty, teasing, sadness, television, family roots, time out for Mom or Dad (or as a couple), minorities, equality, advertising, and of course, tobacco, alcohol and other drugs (the example shown in the video). It is up to you and your family to determine what topic you will discuss each week.

Family talks offer parents an ideal opportunity to discuss their values with their children on a regular basis

Because family talks are based on *topics*, they are really about something very important to most parents: values. Through the use of active communication skills, family talks offer parents an ideal opportunity to discuss their values with their children on a regular basis. Although values cannot be dictated to children, the old saying that "values are caught, not taught" is also misleading. The example we set for our children is certainly important and will help our children "catch" our values. However, values can also be taught to a certain extent by providing information and sound reasoning.

The following tips will help your family talk get off to a smooth start:

1. Plan how you will introduce the topic. Since parents will usually pick the first topic for a family talk, it is helpful to have planned how you will introduce it. Other topics might be chosen by different family members, and each might prepare her own introduction. For example:

"The topic I'd like to introduce for this week's family talk is 'honesty.' Do you remember in the story about the boy who cried wolf, how his making up stories got him into trouble? What happened?"

2. Think of questions that will stimulate discussion. Once you have gotten the talk off the ground, it is usually not difficult to keep the discussion going. Having a few questions prepared to stimulate thinking can help.

Examples:

- Why do you think it is important to be honest?
- How is keeping our agreements a form of honesty?
- How do you feel when someone has lied to you or has not kept an agreement?
- How can we change agreements if we need to?

3. Write down key points you want to make. Influencing our children's values requires accurate information and sound reasoning. With topics such as drugs or sexuality, you may want to do some research on your own to update your knowledge. There are plenty of books and pamphlets that will help. Before having your family talk, write down key points you want to make during the discussion.

Examples:

- The more people trust you, the more they can accept your word without having to check up on you.
- It is easier to keep someone's trust than to win it back once you have lost it.
- The more we trust you, the more freedom we can give you.
- Let's all agree to work hard at keeping our agreements and telling the truth.

4. Find support materials to help provide information or stimulate discussion. There are many materials available to you for use in your family talk: videos, audiocassettes, excerpts from books and magazine articles to name a few. Watching certain television shows together can be a jumping off place for a family talk. Keep your eyes open and you'll find many such resources for making your talks more interesting.

5. Establish ground rules for your talks. Using good communication skills can make the difference between a positive family talk and a failure. Using the

communication principles you've learned in *Active Parenting Today* will help you communicate effectively. Getting agreement from the entire family on communication ground rules can help everyone communicate effectively. You might want to use the following tips as a starting place:

Communication Tips
DO
- speak respectfully.
- invite everyone's ideas.
- share how you think and feel.
- ask yourself how others feel.
- compliment others.

DON'T

- put anyone's ideas down.
- interrupt.
- monopolize the discussion.
- consider only your point of view.
- criticize others.
- call anyone names.

Once you establish ground rules for your family talks, it will be easier to keep everyone in a positive framework. If a child violates one of these rules in a meeting, simply remind him with a firm, calm comment, such as, "Did we agree that we wouldn't criticize each other?"

Problem-Solving Discussions

Helping our children learn to be effective problem solvers will give them a tremendous advantage in a democratic society.

Life is never without problems for very long. It just seems that they go with the territory. So successful people are not those who do not have problems; they are those who are able to find positive solutions to their problems. Helping our children learn to be effective problem solvers will give them a tremendous advantage in a democratic society.

When we first presented the problem-solving model in Chapter Four, we saw that whether the problem was owned by parent or child, it could still be handled in either a problem-solving discussion or in a family council meeting. By teaching our children to work cooperatively as a family in solving such problems we not only equip them to work better with others, but we actually find better solutions to family problems. It really is true that . . .

None of us is as smart as all of us.

The problem-solving discussion can become a regular activity each week, or it can be held as needed by members of the family. It is also used to solve problems during "new business" in the family council meeting. The procedure that will be described here can be used in each case.

Some Ground Rules for Conducting Problem-Solving Discussions

■ **Every person has an equal voice.** Although it is hard for parents to give up some of their authority, problem-solving discussions don't work well unless every person has an equal voice in the decisions made. Every person, including small children, needs to feel that he will be heard and can make a difference in what the family decides to do. Children will not be very enthusiastic about family meetings, nor will they derive much benefit from them, if the meetings are merely forums for parents to decide what everybody will do.

■ **Everyone may share what she thinks and feels about each issue.** It is important that every person at family meetings be encouraged to speak up and say what she thinks and feels about whatever question is on the table. In order to make decisions that are reasonable and fair to everyone, the family needs to hear everyone's opinions and feelings, even the negative ones.

■ **Decisions are made by consensus.** Reaching a consensus means that when there is disagreement, the parties involved discuss the matter until everyone agrees. It does not mean a vote is taken and the majority rules. If an agreement cannot be reached in the meeting, then one of two things may happen: either the matter is tabled until the next meeting when it will be discussed further, or (if it urgently requires decision and action) the parent may exercise his duty as head of the household to make a decision and carry it out.

■ **All decisions are in effect until the next meeting.** Whatever decisions are made at a problem-solving discussion, they should be carried out at least until the next meeting, when they can be discussed again. Complaints after the meeting about decisions made should always bring this answer: "Bring it up again at the next meeting."

■ **Some decisions are reserved for parents to make.** Meeting together does not imply that the parents must always do whatever the children decide to do. Basic questions of health and welfare are parental responsibilities, and the decision is sometimes theirs alone to make. But discussion should always be allowed and encouraged. Sometimes a parent must tell the children of a decision already made. For example, when a parent has been told by her company that a move is required, she can't ask the children for approval. However, the parent can allow them to express their thoughts, concerns and feelings about the move, and to share in the planning.

How To Handle Problems in a Group

The following is a five-step process for solving problems by group discussion:

1. Define the problem. The person with the complaint or the issue to raise is asked to explain it. He should always be asked, "Is this still a problem?" If it is still a problem, the person can be asked simply, "What happened?"

2. Share thoughts and feelings. Persons in the group ask clarifying questions, and reflect back to the complainer what she is saying. At the end of this process, get agreement about the problem. For example, "So we all agree we should all help with household chores." This is the time for family members to share thoughts and feelings about the problem.

3. Generate possible solutions through brainstorming. In "brainstorming," members think of all the possible solutions to a problem, no matter how silly or impractical the solutions may seem. This process is important because ideas generate other ideas; one person's silly idea may contain the seed of a practical solution. To keep the ideas flowing, no one is allowed at this point to say whether the ideas are good or bad. They are simply tossed out into the group without evaluation. The family member who is acting as secretary lists them on paper until no further ideas are forthcoming. Then each idea is discussed.

4. Arrive at a decision through discussion. Every person now has a chance to say what she thinks and feels about each possible solution. Those ideas that are not acceptable to most people are discarded, and discussion focuses on one or two ideas that are thought to be practical. Discussion continues until all people in the group agree on one solution.

5. Put the decision into action. The solution arrived at by brainstorming and discussion is put into effect. In family meetings the solution remains in effect until the next family meeting, when it can be re-evaluated and modified.

The Family Council Meeting

Family talks and problem-solving discussions are useful methods of bringing your family together for specific, time-limited purposes. They may also be incorporated into the family council meeting. The family council meeting offers an ideal forum in which all family members participate in resolving problems and making family decisions.

The family council meeting is a time, once a week, when the entire family gathers to make plans and handle problems that affect family members.

Simply stated, the family council meeting is a time, once a week, when the entire family gathers to make plans and handle problems that affect family members. It can last from 20 minutes to an hour and is conducted according to an agenda. It is in effect what a business meeting is to an organization.

The first family council meeting should be a short one. It's an excellent idea to have only one item of business at this meeting: Plan an outing or a time for fun together right after the meeting. Later meetings can be longer and follow a more extensive agenda.

Leadership Roles

There are two leadership roles at family meetings:

- Chairperson, who keeps the discussion on track and sees that everybody's opinion is heard;
- Secretary, who takes notes during the meeting, writes the minutes after the meeting, and reads the minutes at the next meeting.

These two duties can be assumed by the parents at the first meeting. After that, other family members should take turns at being chairperson and secretary in an agreed-upon order, so that no one person is in charge every time.

Overall Agenda

Here is an agenda that works for many families. We will elaborate on it more in the section "How To Be an Effective Chairperson." You can modify it to fit your circumstances.

1. Compliments
2. Minutes
3. Old business/new business
4. Allowances
5. Treat or family activity

New Business Agenda

A sheet of paper labeled "Agenda" can be taped to the refrigerator or posted at another convenient location.

Most families find that the new business section of the family meeting works better if items have been written on a posted agenda before the meeting. A sheet of paper labeled "Agenda" can be taped to the refrigerator or posted at another convenient location. When a problem occurs that a family member would like handled at the next family meeting, she writes it on the agenda. Example:

Agenda

1. Why can't I spend the night with Dawn? (Sara)
2. Sara comes into my room without asking. (Ramon)
3. Help with chores. (Mom)

Agenda items are handled in order at the next family meeting. Items that are not brought up before the meeting is over can be carried over to the next meeting. Many times, an agenda item will have been handled by those involved before the meeting and can be dropped from the list.

One final benefit of having a written agenda is that it offers parents an excellent way of staying out of children's fights. When a child tries to engage you in solving one of his problems, you can sympathetically suggest that it be put on the agenda for this week's meeting.

Megan: *"Ben keeps taking my toys without asking. Tell him to stop."*

Mother: *"Gee, honey, you sound pretty angry about that. Why don't you put it on the agenda for this week's family meeting?"*

The ground rules for handling this type of problem during a family council meeting are exactly the same as during a problem-solving discussion. You can also use the same five steps for solving problems in a group that were presented on pages 149 and 150. When there are no pressing problems on the new business agenda, you may choose to use this time for a family talk.

How To Be an Effective Chairperson: A Guide for Family Members

Just follow the agenda:

1. Compliments. Ask if anyone appreciates something a family member said or did during the past week. This is a time for members of the family to say thanks to each other for good deeds and to encourage each other with compliments.

2. Minutes. Ask the person who was secretary last week to read the minutes aloud. The minutes remind everyone of what happened at the last meeting.

3. Old business/new business. Ask the family to talk about any matter that wasn't finished at the last meeting. These unfinished matters are called "old business." Let each person say what he or she wants to say, but remind people that they should not talk when someone else is talking.

Next, ask the family to talk about matters that have been written on the agenda. You should read pages 149 and 150 to learn a good method of solving problems that may come up.

4. Allowances. This is the time for Mom or Dad to pass out allowances.

5. Treat or family activity. End the meeting by saying, "The meeting is adjourned." People get tired if meetings go on too long, so keep your meeting to an agreed-upon time limit. We recommend 10-15 minutes with younger children (5- to 7-year-olds) and increasing to 30-45 minutes with older children. Usually, your family will want to have a game or a dessert after the meeting so you can end on a positive note.

How To Be an Effective Secretary: A Guide for Family Members

To be an effective secretary, you need to do only three things:

1. Listen carefully to what is said.
2. Write down what is decided on each matter that is discussed.
3. Later (after the meeting), write a summary of what was decided. This summary is called "the minutes." Read the minutes aloud at the next meeting.

Here is what the minutes may look like:

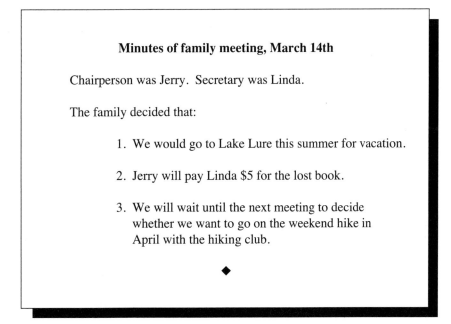

Minutes of family meeting, March 14th

Chairperson was Jerry. Secretary was Linda.

The family decided that:

1. We would go to Lake Lure this summer for vacation.

2. Jerry will pay Linda $5 for the lost book.

3. We will wait until the next meeting to decide whether we want to go on the weekend hike in April with the hiking club.

◆

Family Enrichment Activity

Emphasizing the Family Unit

It is our belief in *Active Parenting Today* that families are the backbone of civilization and that your family is the most important family in the world . . . to your children. History has proven time after time that alone we could never survive, but by forming small cooperative units we could thrive. Families have been a source of belonging, learning and contributing for children and for society—and, to a large extent, the measure of any civilization rests on the strength of its families.

So whether you are part of a traditional Mom and Dad family, or whether it's a blended stepfamily, a single parent family, or any other style of family, it's important for you to look for ways to let your children know that they are part of a family unit. Plan frequent family activities; use phrases like "in our family," and develop your own family traditions and rituals. And give your children the gift of memories by telling and retelling the special stories of your family's history—stories that make your family unique.

Remember, too, that through your family your children will learn that they belong to a much larger family, the family of humankind. And since their contributions to that family will help determine "the future of the people," your job as a parent may very well be the most important job in the world.

The Job of My Life

Sometimes I wonder what to say
To make it better
To make it okay.

Sometimes I wonder just what to do,
Where to take a stand,
And how to help them through

Through the tough times and the glad times
The time we share as a family.

It's not long
The time we have together
Together as a family.

Active Parenting
The most important job in my life.

Active Parenting
Helped me do the job of my life.

And so I'm giving it all I can.
I'm a special part of a special plan.

And joy is growing within my heart
For my precious child
As we make this start.

Active Parenting
The most important job in my life.

Active Parenting
Helped me do the job of my life.

Long ago, we didn't know what challenges lay ahead
But now the joy is real,
And it's such a different feel
To love this child with my eyes opened wide.

Learning more each day
About the Active Parenting way

Active Parenting
The most important job in my life.

Active Parenting
Helped me do the job of my life.

Active Parenting
Helped me do the job of my life.

Planning Your Family Talk

Topic _____

How will you introduce the topic? _____

_____

_____

Questions to open discussion:

1. _____

_____

2. _____

_____

3. _____

_____

4. _____

_____

Key points to make during the discussion:

1. _____

_____

2. _____

_____

3. _____

_____

4. _____

_____

Problem-Solving Discussion Guide Sheet

Whether you have a separate problem-solving discussion or have one during the "new business" section of a family council meeting, the following guide sheet can help you use this process effectively:

What is the problem? _____

_____

What are some of the thoughts and feelings family members have about the problem? _____

_____

_____

What are some possible solutions the family brainstormed? _____

_____

_____

Which solution did the family decide on? _____

_____

_____

How will you follow up to make sure the solution is being put into action? _____

_____

_____

What did you like about the process? _____

_____

_____

What will you do differently next time? _____

_____

Family Council Evaluation

Like any new skill, holding a family council meeting is likely to feel a bit awkward the first time you try it. To help you learn from your first experience this week, fill in the following evaluation after your family council meeting.

How did you introduce the idea of a family meeting to your children? _____

_____

_____

How did they respond? _____

_____

_____

How were you able to enlist their cooperation? (If you were unsuccessful, what happened?) _____

_____

_____

What were the positives in the meeting? _____

_____

_____

What were the problems? _____

_____

_____

What did you like about how you handled the meeting? _____

_____

_____

What will you do differently next time? _____

_____

_____

Chapter Six. Home Activities Checklist

(Check when completed.)

❏ 1. Read Chapter Six.

❏ 2. Complete the Family Enrichment Activity: Look for ways to emphasize your family unit.

❏ 3. Have a problem-solving discussion as part of a family council meeting or by itself, completing the guide sheet on page 157.

❏ 4. Have a family council meeting, completing the evaluation on page 158.

❏ 5. Have a family talk about tobacco, alcohol and other drugs using the optional booklet *Active Parenting Family Guide: Tobacco, Alcohol and Other Drugs,* if appropriate.

❏ 6. Remember that "mistakes are for learning." Be forgiving of yourself and continue to practice all your *Active Parenting Today* skills. Encourage, encourage, encourage yourself!

Notes _____

_____

_____

_____

_____

_____

_____

_____

_____

_____

_____

OSAP Roles for "Parent Training Is Prevention" of Alcohol and Other Drugs

The Office of Substance Abuse Prevention (OSAP) suggests these 10 roles that parents can play in the prevention of drug use.

1. Parents as role models.
Be a positive role model. Children learn best by example.

2. Parents as educators on information resources.
Be informed about alcohol, tobacco and other drugs, and share this with your child.

3. Parents as policy makers and rule setters.
Make a "no use" rule—"No use of illegal drugs by anyone in the family, and no use of alcohol or nicotine by anyone under the legal age"—and enforce it.

4. Parents as stimulators of and participants in healthy activities.
Encourage your child to take part in hobbies, school activities and sports. Get involved yourself; plan fun family activities.

5. Parents as consultants and educators on peer pressure.
"Just say no" is easier said than done. Teach your child to resist peer pressure without feeling foolish.

6. Parents as monitors and supervisors.
Set and enforce curfews; know where your children are.

7. Parents as collaborators with other parents.
Join with other parents to gain support and new ideas. There's strength in numbers.

8. Parents as identifiers and confronters of drug use.
Know how to identify drug use and confront your child when necessary.

9. Parents as managers of intoxicated children.
Get immediate medical help when your child is semi-conscious or unconscious or if you are in doubt.

10. Parents as managers of their own feelings.
Don't blow up; don't give up. You're not guilty.

Active Parenting Publishers has additional resources to help parents with

Parenting Skills

Self-Esteem Development

&

Loss Education

For more information, visit:

www.ActiveParenting.com

Notes